最新時事テーマ収録
Readings for ADVANCED English Learners

Cutting Edge

ナビブック 付

速読トレーニング
文構造解説
重要語句

最難関大対応

Black

本書は、入試最難関レベルの英文読解力を段階的に養成できるように編集されています。

英文素材について

① 新しい素材で、「読む価値がある英文」であること
② 文系・理系のテーマのバランスを取ること
③ 難易度にバラつきがでないこと

を基準に厳選しました。そうして選ばれた英文を、段階的に最難関大入試レベルの読解力を養成できるように配列しています。

設問について

「構文・語彙」など入試の設問になりやすい部分と、内容理解のポイントとなる部分に、英文の流れに沿って設問を配置しています。設問をはじめから解いていくことで、内容が理解できる構成になっています。

「Navi Book」について

　英文学習をより深く、より効率的なものにするためにも付属「Navi Book」の活用をおすすめいたします。「Navi Book」では英文内の重要語句がレベル別にほぼ全て網羅されています。また「英単語」→「日本語の意味」の順で読み上げている音声と一緒に確認することで、より効果的な学習ができるようになっています。英文中の分かりづらい構文や複雑な文構造についても解説していますので、わからなかった英文については問題を解いた後にしっかりと確認しましょう。加えて、国公立大学二次試験に必須の「要約力」、「記述力」を養える要約問題も用意しています。

背景情報について

　英文を読む上で、その英文の中で扱われている内容についての知識があることは大きな武器になります。本書では「テーマ解説」を用意しています。テーマの背景情報だけでなく、ウラ話、さらに入試情報なども織り交ぜた、読み応えのある内容になっています。

【本書の設問について】

設問指示文右端の大学名は、出題校で実際に出題された問題、改は一部改題の問題です。その他の設問は、出題傾向、難易度、記述・客観のバランスに合わせて作成されたオリジナル問題です。

CONTENTS

(1)An elephant should run faster than a horse — at least in theory. That's because big creatures have more of the type of muscle cells used for acceleration. Yet mid-sized animals are the fastest on Earth, a trend that researchers have long struggled to explain. Now, an analysis of nearly 500 species ranging from fruit flies to whales has an answer: The muscle cells in big animals run out of fuel before the creatures can reach their theoretical maximum speed. The work may also help scientists come up with estimates for the running speeds of certain dinosaurs.

Previous studies of animal speed have focused only on certain groups of animals, such as mammals. But that premise often looks at creatures within a limited size range, says Myriam Hirt, a zoologist at the German Centre for Integrative Biodiversity Research in Leipzig. That approach may also hide underlying factors by focusing on animals that are closely related, she notes.

To get around those limitations, (2)Hirt and her colleagues looked at previously collected data for a wide variety of creatures, including ectotherms (so-called cold-blooded animals) as well as warm-blooded endotherms. The 474 species they considered included runners, swimmers, and flyers that ranged in weight from 30 micrograms to 100 tons.

When the scientists mapped★ a creature's top speed versus its weight, they got an inverted-U-shaped graph, with moderately sized animals on top, they report today in *Nature Ecology and Evolution*. On the largest scale, (3)the trend doesn't seem to be related to biomechanics, or how an animal's body parts are arranged and how its joints function, among other factors, Hirt says.

Instead, it appears to be related to a much more fundamental metabolic★ constraint: the length of time required for the animal to reach its theoretical maximum speed, based on the number of "fast-twitch★" muscle fiber cells in the creature's muscles, as compared to the length of time it takes for those cells to run out of readily available energy. ("Fast-twitch" muscle fibers contract more quickly than "slow-twitch★" fibers and generate more force more quickly, but they also fatigue more quickly.) According to the researchers' notion, (4)the "fast-twitch" muscle fibers in immense creatures such as elephants and whales run out of cellular fuel long before they can reach max speed based on the overall number of such fibers.

The study is also a good starting point for revealing other factors that influence a creature's maximum speed, says Christofer Clemente, an ecophysiologist at the University of the Sunshine Coast in Maroochydore, Australia, who wasn't involved in the research. One such unexplained trend is that warm-blooded land animals are ³⁵ usually faster than cold-blooded creatures of comparable size, whereas at sea (5)<u>the reverse</u> is usually true.

   ★　map「マッピングする（値を座標に配置する）」　metabolic「代謝の」　fast-twitch「急激に収縮する」
   slow-twitch「ゆっくり収縮する」

1　下線部（1）を日本語に直しなさい。 (新潟大・改)

2　下線部（2）に関し、Hirt たちの研究方法とそれ以前の研究方法の違いを、本文に即して日本語で簡潔に説明しなさい。

3　下線部（3）に関し、以下の質問に答えなさい。

（ア）　the trend の意味内容を日本語で簡潔に説明しなさい。

（イ）　本文の内容と一致するように、下記の英文の下線部に入る語句（6語以内）を文中から抜き出して書きなさい。

   It seems that the trend is related not to biomechanics but to ------------------------------------

   -- .

4　下線部（4）を日本語に直しなさい。 (新潟大)

次ページへ続く→

5 下線部（5）の内容を、句読点を含めて 40 字以内の日本語で述べなさい。 （新潟大）

										10									20

6 本文の内容と一致するものを 2 つ選びなさい。

① If the muscles used for acceleration were all that mattered, an elephant would have a faster maximum speed than a horse.

② Hirt and her colleagues captured 474 species on their own and mapped each animal's top speed versus its weight.

③ The new study shows that mid-sized creatures are the fastest on Earth because they have more "fast-twitch" muscle fibers than "slow-twitch" fibers.

④ Muscle strength alone does not determine the top velocity of an animal because it can only accelerate for as long as it can draw from available energy stored in muscle fibers.

⑤ The researchers applied the technique they used for the analysis of the 474 living species to the estimates for the running speeds of certain long-extinct dinosaurs.

Memo

Chapter 2

Many linguists predict that at least half of the world's 6,000 or so languages will be ⦿1-11 dead or dying by the year 2050. Languages are becoming extinct at twice the rate of endangered mammals and four times the rate of endangered birds. If this trend continues, the world of the future could be dominated by a dozen or fewer languages.

5　Even higher rates of linguistic devastation are possible. Michael Krauss, director of ⦿1-12 the Alaska Native Language Center, suggests that as many as 90 percent of languages could become moribund or extinct by 2100. According to Krauss, 20 percent to 40 percent of languages are already moribund, and only 5 percent to 10 percent are "safe" in the sense of being widely spoken or having official status. If people "become wise 10　and turn it around," Krauss says, the number of dead or dying languages could be more like 50 percent by 2100 and that's the best-case scenario.

The definition of a healthy language is one that acquires new speakers. No matter ⦿1-13 how many adults use the language, if it isn't passed to the next generation, its fate is already sealed. Although a language may continue to exist for a long time as a second 15　or ceremonial language, it is moribund as soon as children stop learning it. For example, out of twenty native Alaskan languages, only two are still being learned by children.

Although language extinction is sad for the people involved, why should the rest of us care? What effect will other people's language loss have on the future of people who speak English, for example? (A)Replacing a minor language with a more widespread 20　one may even seem like a good thing, allowing people to communicate with each other more easily. But language diversity is as important as biological diversity.

Andrew Woodfield, director of the Centre for Theories of Language and Learning ⦿1-14 in Bristol, England, suggested in a 1995 seminar on language conservation that people do not yet know all the ways in which linguistic diversity is important. "The fact is, no 25　one knows exactly what riches are hidden inside the less-studied languages," he says.

Woodfield compares one argument for conserving unstudied endangered plants — that they may be medically valuable — with the argument for conserving endangered languages. "We have inductive evidence based on past studies of well-known languages that there will be riches, even though we do not know what they will be. (B)It seems 30　paradoxical but it's true. By allowing languages to die out, the human race is destroying things it doesn't understand," he argues.

Stephen Wurm, in his introduction to the Atlas of the World's Languages in Danger ⦿1-15 of Disappearing, tells (C)the story of one medical cure that depended on knowledge of a traditional language. Northern Australia experienced an outbreak of severe skin ulcers★ that resisted conventional treatment. Aborigines★ acquainted with the nurse told her about a lotion derived from a local medicinal plant that would cure the ulcers. Being a woman of broad experience, the woman didn't dismiss this claim for non-Western medical knowledge. Instead, she applied the lotion, which healed the ulcers.

This incident and similar ones have resulted in a general search throughout Australia for medicinal plants known to aboriginal people through their languages and traditional cultures. The search has to be fast because most Australian languages are dying. When they go, the medical knowledge stored in them will go too.

As Michael Krauss expresses it, the web of languages is a "microcosm of highly specialized information. (D)Every language has its own take on the world. One language is not simply a different set of words for the same things." Just as we depend on biological complexity for our physical survival, we depend on linguistic complexity for our cultural survival.

★ skin ulcers「皮膚炎」 Aborigines「原住民」

1 設問の答えとして最も適切なものを、それぞれ１つずつ選びなさい。

(1) **From the passage it may be inferred that** _____   (上智大)

① there are more languages dying than endangered animals.
② languages are dying more quickly than endangered animals.
③ one half of the world's languages will have died by 2050.
④ the number of dead languages will definitely double in the future.

(2) **If worse comes to worst, about how many languages would still be in existence by the end of this century?**   (上智大)

① 3000   ② 1200   ③ 600   ④ 10

(3) **A language can be considered 'safe'** _____   (上智大)

① if it is recognized as a national language.
② if it is spoken by at least 5 percent of the population.
③ if its speakers are wise.
④ if it is not already moribund.

次ページへ続く→

2 下線部（A）を日本語に直しなさい。

....
....
....

3 下線部（B）の指す内容を日本語で述べなさい。

....
....
....

4 下線部（C）に関し、以下の設問に日本語で答えなさい。

（1） 話の内容を簡潔に日本語でまとめなさい。

....
....
....

（2） 話が示唆していることを、本文に即して述べなさい。

....
....

5 下線部（D）の意味を、日本語でわかりやすく述べなさい。

....

6 次の設問の答えとして最も適切なものを１つ選びなさい。　　　　　　（上智大）

What would be the best title of this chapter?

①　The Different Worlds of Human Language
②　The Death of Languages — a Natural Phenomenon
③　The Loss of an Endangered Language, a Grave Loss for Medicine
④　Conserving Endangered Languages — Protecting Mankind's Treasures

Memo

A sari for a month. It shouldn't have been a big deal but it was. After all, I had 🔊1-21 grown up around women wearing saris in India. My mother even slept in one.

In India, saris are adult clothes. After I turned eighteen, I occasionally wore a beautiful sari for weddings and holidays and to the temple. But wearing a silk sari to an Indian party was one thing. Deciding to wear a sari every day while living in New York, especially after ten years in Western clothes, seemed (1)outrageous, even to me.

The sari is six yards of fabric folded into a graceful yet impractical garment. It is fragile and can fall apart at any moment. When worn right, it is supremely elegant and feminine.

It requires (2a), however. No longer could I spring across the street just before 🔊1-22 the light changed. The sari forced me to shorten my strides. I had to throw my shoulders back and pay attention to my posture. I couldn't squeeze into a crowded subway car for fear that someone would accidentally pull my sari. I couldn't balance four bags from the supermarket in one hand and pull out my house keys from a convenient pocket with the other. By the end of the first week, I was feeling frustrated and angry with myself. What was I trying to (3a)?

The notion of wearing a sari every day was relatively new for me. During my 🔊1-23 college years — the age when most girls in India begin wearing saris regularly — I was studying in America as an art student and I wore casual clothes just as other students did. After getting married, I became a housewife experimenting with more fashionable clothes. Over the years, in short, I tried to talk, walk, and act like an (4).

Then I moved to New York and became a mother. I wanted to teach my three- 🔊1-24 year-old daughter Indian values and traditions because I knew she would be profoundly different from the children she would play with in religion (we are Hindus), eating habits (we are vegetarians), and the festivals we celebrated. (A)Wearing a sari every day was my way of showing her that she could melt into the pot while keeping her individual flavor.

It wasn't just for my daughter's sake that I decided to wear a sari. I was tired of 🔊1-25 trying to (3b). No American singers had ever spoken to me as deeply as my favorite Indian singers. Nor could I sing popular American songs as easily as I could my favorite Indian tunes. Much as I enjoyed American food, I couldn't last four days without an Indian meal. It was time to show my ethnicity with a sari and a bright red bindi★. I was going to be an (5a), but on my own terms. It was America's turn to adjust to me.

Slowly, I eased into wearing the garment. I owned it and it owned me. Strangers 🔊1-26 stared at me as I walked proudly across a crowded bookstore. Some of them caught my eye and smiled. At first, I resented being an (5b). Then I wondered: perhaps I reminded them of a wonderful holiday in India or a favorite Indian cookbook. Shop assistants pronounced their words clearly when they spoke to me. Everywhere, I was stopped with questions about India as if wearing a sari had made me an (5c). One Japanese lady near Times Square asked to have her picture taken with me. (B)<u>A tourist had thought that I was one, too, just steps from my home.</u>

1-27　　But there were unexpected (2b). Indian taxi drivers raced across lanes and stopped in front of me just as I stepped into the street to hail a cab. When my daughter climbed high up the jungle gym in Central Park, I gathered my sari and prepared to follow, hoping it wouldn't balloon out like Marilyn Monroe's dress. One of the dads standing nearby saw that I was in trouble and volunteered to climb after her. (6)<u>A knight in New York?</u> Was it me? Or was it my sari?

1-28　　Best of all, my family approved. My husband praised me. My parents were proud of me. My daughter gave out a sigh of admiration when I pulled out my colorful saris. When I hugged her tenderly in my arms, scents from the small bag of sweet-smelling herbs that I used to freshen my sari at night escaped from the folds of cloth and calmed her to sleep. (C)<u>I felt part of a long line of Indian mothers who had rocked their babies this way.</u>

1-29　　Soon, the month was over. My self-imposed (2c) was coming to an end. Instead of feeling liberated, I felt a sharp pain of unease. I had started to (3c) my sari.

　　Saris were impractical for America, I told myself. I would continue to wear them but not every day. It was time to go back to my sensible casual clothes.

　　★　bindi「ヒンドゥー教徒の女性が額につける印」

1　下線部（1）の言い換えとして最も適切なものを1つ選びなさい。

　　①　extreme　　　②　gorgeous　　　③　hostile　　　④　precious　　　⑤　serious

2　空所（2a）〜（2c）を埋めるのに最も適切なものを1つずつ選びなさい。ただし、同じ番号を複数回使わないこと。　　　　　　　　　　　　　　　　　　　　　　　　　　　　　　（東京大）

　　①　advantages　　②　assistance　　③　attempts　　④　convenience　　⑤　feelings
　　⑥　helplessness　　⑦　information　　⑧　obligation　　⑨　opportunity　　⑩　sacrifices

3　空所（3a）〜（3c）を埋めるのに最も適切なものを1つずつ選びなさい。ただし、同じ番号を複数回使わないこと。　　　　　　　　　　　　　　　　　　　　　　　　　　　　　　（東京大）

　　①　avoid　　　②　enjoy　　　③　fit in　　　④　insist　　　⑤　prove　　　⑥　put on

次ページへ続く→

4 空所（4）に入る最も適切な1語を書きなさい。ただし、文中に使われている語であること。

---

5 空所（5a）〜（5c）を埋めるのに最も適切な組み合わせを1つ選びなさい。 （東京大）

① authority / exhibit / immigrant   ② authority / immigrant / exhibit

③ exhibit / authority / immigrant   ④ exhibit / immigrant / authority

⑤ immigrant / authority / exhibit   ⑥ immigrant / exhibit / authority

6 下線部（6）の説明として最も適切なものを1つ選びなさい。 （東京大）

① She is amazed that a man would be kind enough to help a stranger in New York.

② She is surprised that a man of noble birth would act so bravely in New York.

③ She wonders if men have many opportunities to help beautiful women in New York.

④ She is confused by a father putting her daughter before his own children in New York.

⑤ She is shocked at a man's eagerness to get to know someone who looks so different in New York.

7 下線部（A）を日本語に直しなさい。

---

8 下線部（B）を日本語に直しなさい。ただし、one が何を指すか明らかにすること。 （東京大）

---

9 下線部（C）を日本語に直しなさい。

---

10 本文の内容と一致するものを1つ選びなさい。 （東京大）

① The writer decided to wear saris because she wanted to express her Indian identity.

② The sari was so elegant and feminine that the writer naturally behaved gracefully.

③ Despite her initial reluctance to wear saris, the writer gradually became an expert on India.

④ Shop assistants spoke to the writer very politely because they saw her in a sari and thought she should be treated with respect.

Memo

How do migrating birds find their way? First we must ask, what possible clues are ⊙1-34 there? If birds are flying over land, where there are features below that are distinct and stay the same for year after year — rivers, roads, forests, coastlines — then, of course, they can use their eyes. There is plenty of evidence that (1)birds do just this. Many, for 5 example, follow coastlines and thread their way through straits and mountain passes.

When they get very close to where they want to be, many use their sense of smell. ⊙1-35 Homing pigeons give a clue to this. ("Homing" is not the same as migration. It suggests that pigeons can find their way home when taken by train or truck to some far-distant place and then released. But homing surely has some of the same mechanisms as 10 migration does, and so can give clues to how it works.) It seems that as pigeons get fairly close to their home, they first pick up general smells that tell of bird dwellings — perhaps the general tempting stink of ammonia. As they get nearer, the smells become more specifically pigeon-like. Finally, as they get very close, they recognize the very particular odor of their own flock in its own space. More and more evidence is revealing that 15 humans, too, have a wonderful awareness of odor, even if they do not consciously recognize it, such that they find particular men or women attractive or disgusting according to their primitive substances such as sweat: no doubt a cooling thought for those who like to suppose that (2)human beings have risen above such things. We do not normally think of birds as creatures that attach importance to smell, but many of them 20 do, in many contexts.

But what use are (A) clues when a bird is above some apparently boundless ocean? ⊙1-36 What value is (B) when it is a thousand miles from where it wants to be? What else is there?

Quite a lot, is the answer. On the visual front, there is the sun by day and the moon ⊙1-37 25 and stars by night. These are hard to make good use of unless the bird also has some sense of time, so it knows where the sun or the moon ought to be at a particular time; but birds do have a sense of time.

Human beings navigate by the heavenly bodies, too, but we make a great science of it. ⊙1-38 The skills of the navigator were among the most complex and prized in all the world's 30 navies until well into the nineteenth century, when sailors in danger could find out where they were by radio. Traditional long-distance sailors needed telescopes and charts, and pages and pages of tables, to help them work out where they were. Birds have to do all this in their heads, in their bird brains, on the wing. The problem conceptually is the same as we meet in discussing the diving of fish-eating seabirds (how they always fold their wings at exactly the right time). In each case the math is immensely complicated, ₃₅ once you spell it out. But presumably birds on the wing, not familiar with mathematics, don't spell it out. (3)<u>They must have some practical rules that instantly translate the cues that are offered by the sun and stars and moon into directives for purposeful action.</u>

1-39   Again, there are clues and stories that seem to be throwing some light. For instance, (4)<u>many kinds of birds are known to use star maps</u>. In the early weeks of life the baby ₄₀ birds sit in their nests and study the night sky — and are somewhat confused if those early weeks are too cloudy. But they do not, as human amateur astronomers might do, spend their time learning the individual constellations★ — how to recognize Orion★ or trace the fanciful outline of Taurus★, or whatever. Instead, they focus on the part that does not move as the night progresses, which in the Northern Hemisphere means the ₄₅ North Star. They can see, if they look at it long enough, that as the night progresses, all the stars in the sky, including the mighty Orion and the notional Taurus, seem to revolve around the Pole Star, which sits in the middle like the central part of a giant cartwheel. Once they recognize the central part, the most fundamental problem is solved. The creature that can do this knows where north is and everything else can be figured out. I ₅₀ don't know what the equivalent would be in the Southern Hemisphere, but undoubtedly there is one. Navigation simply does not seem to need the details of astronomy.

   ★ constellation「星座」 Orion「オリオン座」 Taurus「牡牛座」

1 下線部（1）の内容を具体的に日本語で説明しなさい。

....
....

2 第1、2段落の内容から判断して、空所（A）（B）に入る英語1語を、本文中から抜き出しなさい。

(A) .... 　　　(B) ....

3 下線部（2）について、筆者が言おうとしていることを、本文に即して具体的に日本語で説明しなさい。

(東北大)

....
....
....

次ページへ続く→

4 下線部（3）を日本語に直しなさい。 （東北大）

....

....

....

5 下線部（4）に関し、鳥は star maps から何を学び、またそれをどのように利用しているか、本文の内容に即して日本語で述べなさい。

....

....

....

....

6 本文の内容と一致するものを 2 つ選びなさい。

① Migrating birds find their way mainly by using their eyes and they seldom use their sense of smell.

② While many of the birds have a fine sense of smell, we human beings have long since lost it and cannot recognize the particular odor that each of us has.

③ Though birds don't have telescopes or charts or pages of tables or radio, they use the cues given by the sun and stars and moon and can work out where they are.

④ The baby birds first try to learn the movement of all the stars in the sky but soon find it impossible because there are too many cloudy nights.

⑤ Studying the night sky, birds find one unmoving star in the center of the movement of stars, which is the North Star in the Northern Hemisphere, and they know where north is.

Memo

Chapter 5

The distribution of educational opportunity plays a key role in shaping human development prospects. Within countries, governments and people increasingly recognize that unequal opportunities for education are linked to inequalities in income, health and wider life chances. And (1)what is true within countries is true also between countries. Large global gaps in education reinforce the extreme divides between rich and poor nations in income, health and other aspects of human development.

The full extent of the gulf in opportunities for education is not widely appreciated. Education is a universal human right. However, enjoyment of that right is heavily conditioned by birth and inherited circumstance. Access to education is greatly influenced by where one is born and by other factors over which children have no control, including parental income and nationality.

From a global perspective, being born in a developing country is a strong indicator for reduced opportunity. (2)School achievement, measured in terms of the average number of years or grade reached in education, is one (admittedly limited) measure of global inequality. While almost all member countries of the Organisation for Economic Co-operation and Development (OECD) have attained universal school achievement to grade 9, most countries in developing regions are far from this position. At age 16, over 80% of the population of the OECD countries is in secondary school while one-quarter of sub-Saharan★ Africa's population is still in primary school. Four years later, at age 20, around 30% of the OECD population is in post-secondary education. The figure for sub-Saharan Africa is 2%.

(3)Striking as they are, these figures tell only part of the story. One way of thinking about unequal opportunity is to consider the chance that a child born in one country will achieve a given level of education relative to a child born somewhere else. The results are revealing. They show that children in countries such as Mali and Mozambique have less chance of completing primary school than children in France or the United Kingdom have of reaching higher education. The gulf in attainment is not restricted to sub-Saharan Africa. Around one in five pupils entering primary school in Latin America and in South and West Asia does not survive to the last primary grade.

Global inequalities in education mirror inequalities in income. The association is not coincidental. While the relationship between education and wealth creation is complex, knowledge has an important influence on economic growth and productivity. In an increasingly knowledge-based international economy, differences in educational opportunities are taking on more importance. (4)There is a growing sense in which today's inequalities in education can be seen as a predictor for tomorrow's inequalities in the global distribution of wealth, and in opportunities for health and employment. (5)The fact that in half the countries of sub-Saharan Africa the survival rate to the last grade of primary school is 67% or less is not irrelevant to prospects for overcoming the region's marginalization in the global economy.

* sub-Saharan「サハラ以南の」

1 下線部（1）の内容を、本文に即して日本語で簡潔に説明しなさい。

---

2 下線部（2）を日本語に直しなさい。 (京都大)

---

3 下線部（3）を日本語に直しなさい。 (京都大)

---

4 下線部（4）を日本語に直しなさい。

---

5 下線部（5）を日本語に直しなさい。 (京都大)

Abraham Darby arrived in Coalbrookdale★ with a mission in mind: to produce ◉1-53
cheap iron using coal — in the form of coke — as a fuel. His success was foundational
to the Industrial Revolution, allowing the production of less expensive iron and so
enabling the construction of railways, steamships and industrial machinery, not to
mention the famous iron bridge built by Darby's grandson near Coalbrookdale. A
stroke of genius?

(1)Hardly. Economic historian Robert Allen points out that Darby's pivotal invention ◉1-54
was a simple response to economic incentives. Existing iron smelters★ used wood; it
did not need an Einstein to think of chucking★ coal in the furnace★ instead. What it
required was a supply of the world's cheapest coal to make the project worthwhile, and
that is exactly what Coalbrookdale's mines provided. Once he worked out that the
economics were viable, Darby simply commissioned researchers to experiment, solve
the technical problems, and make (2)his project a reality. And even after Darby's
invention was tried and tested, it did not spread to mainland Europe, for the simple
reason that Europe's coal was too expensive; most of it was shipped over from Newcastle
in England anyway. Coke smelting in France or Germany was technologically possible,
but just not profitable for 150 years.

This seems like an unusually straightforward case, but on closer inspection the ◉1-55
same turns out to be true of many of the Industrial Revolution's technological advances.
Cotton-spinning machinery, for example, did not require any scientific knowledge, just
a careful process of development and experimentation plus a little creativity: (3)legend
has it that the spinning jenny★ was inspired by a traditional medieval spinning wheel
that fell over and kept spinning while lying on the ground. The inventors of spinning
machines such as the spinning jenny and the water frame★ launched serious research
programs; they knew exactly what they hoped to achieve, and just needed to solve a
series of modest engineering problems.

(4)They expended this considerable effort rationally — and those in France or ◉1-56
China rationally did not — because (5)the financials added up: Allen's calculations show
that British workers were at that time the most highly paid in the world, whether
measured against the price of silver, of food, of energy, or of capital. That meant that
they were big consumers of imported cotton, but also that a labour-saving device would
pay dividends★. In Britain, a spinning jenny cost less than five months' wages, while

in low-wage France it cost more than a year's wages. It was cheap French labour that accounted for the machine's slow adoption on the continent, not the superior scientific ingenuity of the British. 35

1-57　　That was even more true of steam engines. They were, unusually for Industrial Revolution technology, based on an actual scientific advance: Galileo discovered that atmosphere had weight and so could exert pressure. Yet the practical invention took place in Britain, not in Galileo's Italy, and again, the reason was not genius but the fact that labour was expensive and fuel was incredibly cheap. Allen calculates that, in terms 40 of thermal units* per hour, wages in Newcastle in those days were perhaps ten times higher than those in continental cities such as Paris and Strasbourg. Labour in China was even cheaper. By the same reckoning, London wages were three times higher than those in continental cities and six or seven times those in Beijing. (6)It's no surprise that the steam engine, a device for replacing labour with coal, was a British invention. 45

1-58　　All this shows that many of the important innovations of the Industrial Revolution were calculated and deliberate responses to high British wages and cheap British coal. The cheap coal was an accident of geography, but the wages weren't. Our historical detective story leads us to another question: (7)＿＿＿＿＿＿＿＿＿＿＿＿

　　＊　Coalbrookdale　イングランド西部の地名　　smelter「精錬所」　　chuck「投げる」　　furnace「炉」
　　　　spinning jenny「ジェニー紡績機」　　water frame「水力紡績機」　　pay dividends「後で元がとれる」
　　　　thermal unit「熱量単位」

1 下線部（1）が意味する具体的内容を、文脈を踏まえて 20 字以内の日本語で述べなさい。　　(名古屋大)

2 下線部（2）の内容を表す最も適切な連続した 4 語を本文中から英語で抜き出しなさい。　　(名古屋大)

3 下線部（3）を日本語に直しなさい。

4 下線部（4）の内容を表す最も適切な連続した 5 語を本文中から英語で抜き出しなさい。　　(名古屋大)

次ページへ続く→

5 下線部（5）のように言えるのはなぜか、本文に即して日本語で説明しなさい。

6 下線部（6）のように言えるのはなぜか、最も適切な理由を 2 つ、それぞれ 20 字以内の日本語で述べなさい。

（名古屋大）

```
                              10                          20
┌──┬──┬──┬──┬──┬──┬──┬──┬──┬──┬──┬──┬──┬──┬──┬──┬──┬──┬──┐
│  │  │  │  │  │  │  │  │  │  │  │  │  │  │  │  │  │  │  │
├──┼──┼──┼──┼──┼──┼──┼──┼──┼──┼──┼──┼──┼──┼──┼──┼──┼──┼──┤
│  │  │  │  │  │  │  │  │  │  │  │  │  │  │  │  │  │  │  │
└──┴──┴──┴──┴──┴──┴──┴──┴──┴──┴──┴──┴──┴──┴──┴──┴──┴──┴──┘
```

7 下線部（7）に入る最も適切な疑問文を 1 つ選びなさい。

（名古屋大）

① who invented the steam engine?

② what invention came next?

③ where did British coal come from?

④ when did the Industrial Revolution begin?

⑤ why were wages so high?

⑥ how did Abraham Darby die?

8 本文の内容と一致するものを 1 つ選びなさい。

① The famous iron bridge built by Abraham Darby's grandson owed its construction to the production of less expensive iron.

② France and Germany could not produce cheap iron because they were far behind Britain in the development of technology for coke smelting.

③ Spinning jenny was one good example to show the importance of scientific knowledge in many of the important innovations of the Industrial Revolution.

④ Steam engines were first invented in Britain because the country had produced many scientists of genius like Galileo before the Industrial Revolution.

⑤ It was no accident that cheap coal was abundant in Britain and the wages of British workers were high.

Memo

According to Shoshana Zuboff, a professor at the Harvard Business School, 🔊1-63 surveillance★ capitalism originated with the brilliant discoveries and the bold and shameless claims of one American firm: Google.

Incorporated in 1998, Google soon came to dominate Internet search. But initially, 🔊1-64
5 it did not focus on advertising and had no clear path to profitability. What it did have was a completely new insight: the data it derived from searches — the numbers and patterns of questions, their phrasing, people's click patterns, and so on — could be used to improve Google's search results and add new services for users. This would attract more users, which would in turn further improve its search engine in (1)a
10 repeating cycle of learning and expansion.

(2)Google's commercial breakthrough came in 2002, when it saw that it could also 🔊1-65 use the data it collected to profile the users themselves according to their characteristics and interests. Then, instead of matching ads with search questions, the company could match ads with individual users. Targeting ads precisely and efficiently to individuals
15 is the Holy Grail★ of advertising. Rather than being Google's customers, Zuboff argues, the users became its raw-material suppliers, from whom the firm derived what she calls "behavioral surplus." That surplus consists of the data above and beyond what Google needs to improve user services.

(3)Together with the company's formidable capabilities in artificial intelligence, 🔊1-66
20 Google's enormous flows of data enabled it to create what Zuboff sees as the true basis of the surveillance industry — "prediction products," which anticipate what users will do "now, soon, and later." Predicting what people will buy is the key to advertising, but behavioral predictions have obvious value for other purposes, as well, such as insurance, hiring decisions, and political campaigns.

25 Zuboff's analysis helps make sense of (4)the seemingly unrelated services offered 🔊1-67 by Google, its diverse ventures and many acquisitions. Gmail, Google Maps, the Android operating system, YouTube, Google Home, even self-driving cars — these and dozens of other services are all ways, Zuboff argues, of expanding the company's "supply routes" for user data both on- and offline. Asking for permission to obtain
30 those data has not been part of the company's operating style. For instance, when the company was developing Street View, a feature of its mapping service that displays

photographs of different locations, it went ahead and recorded images of streets and homes in different countries without first asking for local permission, fighting off opposition as it arose. In the surveillance business, any undefended area of social life is (5)fair game.

1-68   This pattern of expansion reflects an underlying logic of the industry: in the competition for artificial intelligence and surveillance revenues, the advantage goes to the firms that can acquire both vast and varied streams of data. The other companies engaged in surveillance capitalism at the highest level — Amazon, Facebook, Microsoft, and the big telecommunications companies — also face the same expansionary needs.   40
(6)Step by step, the industry has expanded both the scope of surveillance (by migrating from the virtual into the real world) and the depth of surveillance (by going into the interiors of individuals' lives and accumulating data on their personalities, moods, and emotions).

* surveillance : spying, observation
  Holy Grail : a thing which is eagerly pursued or sought after

1 Regarding the underlined part (1), explain in Japanese what is meant by "a repeating cycle of learning and expansion". (九州大)

----

2 Regarding the underlined part (2), explain in Japanese what "breakthrough" happened at Google in 2002. (九州大)

----

3 Translate the underlined part (3) into Japanese.

次ページへ続く→

4 Regarding the underlined part (4), how does Zuboff's analysis explain "the seemingly unrelated services offered by Google"? Answer <u>in Japanese</u>.

(九州大)

----

5 Which of the following best describes the meaning of the underlined words (5)<u>fair game</u> as used in the text?

① a social activity that is always conducted justly, without fear or favor

② a business field where companies cannot compete on an equal basis

③ a situation in which people involved are not allowed to criticize each other

④ a person or thing that is considered a reasonable target for exploitation or attack

6 Translate the underlined part (6) into Japanese.

----

7 Choose the two statements below which agree with what is written in the passage.

① Soon after its incorporation, Google established the dominant position in advertising as well as in Internet search.

② Zuboff says that Google collects more data than is necessary from its users by matching ads with them.

③ Google found that forecasting users' buying patterns, rather than their behavioral predictions, was a more effective way for advertising.

④ When developing Street View, Google took images of different places without permission to obtain personal data because there was no protest against those practices.

⑤ Google collects huge quantities of data about our behaviors online and in the physical world, which it turns into its products and services.

Memo

The concept of altruism is ready for retirement. 　　　　　　　　⊙2-1

Not that the phenomenon of helping others and doing good to other people is about to go away — not at all. On the contrary, the appreciation of the importance of bonds between individuals is on the rise in the modern understanding of animal and
5 human societies. What needs to go away is the basic idea behind the concept of altruism — that there is a conflict of interest between helping yourself and helping others.

The word "altruism" was coined in the 1850s by the great French sociologist 　⊙2-2
Auguste Comte. What it means is that you do something for other people (the Old
10 French *altrui*, from the Latin *alter*), not just for yourself. Thus, it opposes egoism or selfishness. (1)This concept is rooted in the notion that human beings and animals are dominated by selfishness and egoism, so that you need a concept to explain why they sometimes behave unselfishly and kindly to others.

But the reality is different: Humans are deeply bound to other humans, and most 　⊙2-3
15 actions are reciprocal and in the interest of both (2)parties (or, in the case of hatred, in the disinterest of both). The starting point is neither selfishness nor altruism but the state of being bound together. It's an illusion to believe that you can be happy when no one else is. Or that other people will not be affected by your unhappiness.

Behavioral science and neurobiology have shown how intimately we're bound. 　⊙2-4
20 Phenomena like mimicry*, emotional contagion*, empathy, sympathy, compassion, and prosocial* behavior are evident in humans and animals alike. (3)We're influenced by the well-being of others in more ways than we normally care to think of. Therefore, a simple rule applies: *Everyone feels better when you're well, and you feel better when everyone is well.*

25 This correlated state is the real one. Egoism and its opposite concept, altruism, are 　⊙2-5
unsubstantial concepts — shadows or even illusions. This applies also to the immediate psychological level: If helping others fills you with satisfaction, is it not also in your own interest to help others? Are you not, then, helping yourself? Being kind to others means being (ア).

30 Likewise, if you feel better and make more money when you're generous and 　⊙2-6
contribute to the well-being and resources of other people — as in the welfare societies that, like Scandinavian countries, became rich through sharing and equality — then

whoever wants to keep everything for himself or herself, with no gift-giving, no taxpaying, and no generosity, is just an amateur egoist. (4)<u>Real egoists share.</u>

2-7　　It's not altruistic to be an altruist — just wise. Helping others is in your own interest. We don't need a concept to explain that behavior. Auguste Comte's concept is therefore ready for retirement. We can all just help each other, without wondering why.

* mimicry : the activity or art of copying the behavior or speech of other people
  contagion : the spreading of something bad from person to person
  prosocial : helpful and beneficial for other people and society

1　第 2 段落（Not that ...）では、消え去る必要があるのはどんな考えだと述べているか、40 字以内の日本語で書きなさい。

2　下線部（1）を、This concept の内容を具体的に明らかにしながら日本語に直しなさい。　(九州大・改)

3　下線部（2）の parties の単数形 party の意味の説明として、最も適切なものを 1 つ選びなさい。　(九州大)

① a social gathering of guests, usually involving eating, drinking, and entertainment

② a group that shares the same political views and participates in elections and government

③ a group of people who go somewhere together or do something together

④ a person or a group of people forming one side in an activity

4　文脈から判断して、空所（ア）に入る英語を 3 語で書きなさい。

5　下線部（3）を日本語に直しなさい。　(九州大)

次ページへ続く→

6 下線部（4）について、その理由を日本語で述べなさい。 （九州大）

....

....

7 本文の主旨と一致するものを 1 つ選びなさい。

① "Altruism" is much less appreciated today than in Auguste Comte's age, so it is time to retire this concept.

② We behave selfishly and cannot help others because we are all born egoists, so the concept "altruism" is not necessary.

③ When he invented the word "altruism" in the 1850s, Auguste Comte knew that it would go away some day.

④ We need the concept "altruism" all the more because we are deeply bound to each other.

⑤ Helping others is in our own interest, so we don't need the concept "altruism" to explain why we behave kindly to others.

Memo

Chapter 9

Explaining the world through stories is, of course, nothing new. Stories and 2-12
storytelling are as fundamental to human nature as science, and every culture we have
records of has its creation story and tales of moral instruction. Although our detailed
knowledge of ancient stories extends back only a few thousand years, to the beginnings
5 of written language, human fascination with narrative most likely stretches back much
further. Stone carvings and cave paintings dating back forty thousand years mix
human and animal figures in interesting ways, and it's easy to imagine that there are
stories behind the images.

Indeed, the tendency to seek and invent narrative is a deeply rooted part of human 2-13
10 nature. We see stories everywhere we look. (A)In a classic psychology experiment,
people asked to describe a short animation of geometric shapes moving about a
screen used language that attributed intention to the shapes, as if the objects were
conscious actors: "The red triangle chased the blue circle off the screen."

Young children live in a world with little distinction between fact and story. As I 2-14
15 started writing this book, my four-year-old daughter was going through a superhero
phase. At various times, she identified herself as Strong Girl, Fast Girl, Brave Girl,
Smart Girl, Ninja Girl, and Butterfly Girl, and nearly every day, we heard a new story
of how her heroic actions stopped the various Bad Guys. Now that she's older, her
stories have become more and more involved and are a reliable source of parental
20 entertainment.

This fascination with narrative carries over to explanations of how the world 2-15
works.

(a) These stories generally seem peculiar and almost comical, as modern scientific
explanations of weather in terms of the motion of air and water in the atmosphere
25 are vastly more effective at predicting the course of major storms.

(b) A large chunk of mythology consists of attempts to impose narrative on the
world, by attributing natural phenomena to capricious or revengeful gods and
heroes.

(c) And yet, when a weather disaster does strike, it is virtually (and depressingly)
30 certain that at least one fundamentalist religious leader will attribute it to divine
vengeance for something or another.

Modern superstition operates on a smaller scale, as well. Every newspaper in 2-16

America runs a daily horoscope column, which millions of people read and follow. Otherwise highly educated people will behave as if the motion of distant planets had some significant influence over chance events and interpersonal interactions on Earth. (B)The stubborn persistence of even readily falsifiable ideas like astrology shows the power of the human desire to impose narrative on random events.

◉2-17 (C)Storytelling and even myth making have a place in science, too. In learning about physics, for example, a student can hardly avoid hearing the famous stories of Galileo Galilei's dropping weights off the Leaning Tower of Pisa and Isaac Newton's inventing his theory of gravity when an apple fell on him. Of course, neither of these stories is literally true. There are elements of truth to both — Galileo did careful experiments to demonstrate that light and heavy objects fall at the same rate, and Newton did some of his critical work on gravitation at his family farm, while avoiding a plague outbreak in London. But the colorful and specific stories about the origins of those theories are almost completely fiction. These persist, though, because they are useful. They help fix the key science in the minds of students by embedding the facts within a narrative. A disconnected series of abstract facts and figures is very difficult to remember, but if you can weave those facts into a story, they become easier to remember. The stories of Galileo in the tower and Newton under the apple tree help bring home one of the key early ideas in physics by relying on the power of stories (in fact, most people remember the stories long after they've forgotten the underlying science).

◉2-18 Essentially all successful scientific theories contain an element of narrative: Event A leads to effect B, which explains observation C. (D)Some sciences even have to resist the temptation to impose too much narrative: Evolutionary biologists have struggled for years against the notion that evolution is inherently progressive, working toward some kind of goal. And one of the serious errors of reporting on medical and psychological research is the mistaken assumption that when two phenomena tend to occur together, one phenomenon must cause the other. "Correlation is not causation" is a slogan among scientists and doubters, for good reason.

1 下線部（A）を日本語に直しなさい。 （東北大）

....

....

....

....

次ページへ続く→

2 This fascination with narrative carries over to explanations of how the world works. に続く 3つの文（a）～（c）は原文の順序を変えてある。原文の（a）～（c）の順序を１つ選びなさい。　(東北大)

① （a）−（c）−（b）　　② （b）−（a）−（c）　　③ （b）−（c）−（a）

④ （c）−（a）−（b）　　⑤ （c）−（b）−（a）

3 下線部（B）を日本語に直しなさい。

....

....

....

4 下線部（C）について、筆者がガリレオとニュートンの例を取り上げて述べたかったことは何か、本文に即して日本語で説明しなさい。　(東北大)

....

....

....

....

5 下線部（D）はどのようなことを意味しているか、本文に即して具体例をあげながら日本語で説明しなさい。　(東北大)

....

....

....

....

6 本文の内容と一致するものを１つ選びなさい。

① A few thousand years ago human beings began to record stories in written language, which is the first instance showing human fascination with narrative.

② The writer of this passage is worried that his daughter might not progress to the stage where she can distinguish between fact and story.

③ In the modern society there are no people who think that natural disasters are caused by divine vengeance.

④ Horoscope columns in newspapers are popular among the American population including highly educated people.

⑤ Fictional stories are often used to make it easier for students to remember abstract facts and figures, but most people doubt their effectiveness.

Memo

Why have social anxieties increased so dramatically in many developed countries ⊙2-23 over the last half century, as one American psychologist's studies suggest they have? Why does the 'social evaluative threat' seem so great? (1)A reasonable explanation is the break-up of the settled communities of the past. People used to grow up knowing, and being known by, many of the same people all their lives. Although geographical mobility had been increasing for several generations, the last half century has seen a particularly rapid rise.

At the beginning of this period it was still common for people — in rural and ⊙2-24 urban areas alike — never to have travelled much beyond the boundaries of their immediate city or village community. Married brothers and sisters, parents and grandparents, tended to remain living nearby and the community consisted of people who had often known each other for much of their lives. But now that so many people move from where they grew up, knowledge of neighbours tends to be superficial or non-existent. People's sense of identity used to be rooted in the community to which they belonged, in people's real knowledge of each other, but now it is lost in the facelessness of mass society. Familiar faces have been replaced by a constant flow of strangers. As a result, who we are, identity itself, is endlessly open to question.

The problem is shown even in the difficulty we have in distinguishing between the ⊙2-25 concept of the 'esteem' in which we may or may not be held by others, and our own self-esteem. The evidence of our sensitivity to '(2)social evaluative threat', coupled with the American psychologist's evidence of long-term rises in anxiety, suggests that we may — by the standards of any previous society — have become highly self-conscious, overly concerned with how we appear to others, worried that we might come across as unattractive, boring, ignorant or whatever, and constantly trying to manage the impressions we make. And at the core of our interactions with strangers is our concern at the social judgements and evaluations they might make: how do they rate us, did we give a good account of ourselves? This insecurity is part of the modern psychological condition.

Greater (3) between people seems to heighten their social evaluation anxieties ⊙2-26 by increasing the importance of social status. Instead of accepting each other as equals on the basis of our common humanity as we might in more equal settings, measuring each other's worth becomes more important as status differences widen.

We come to see social position as a more important feature of a person's identity. Between strangers (4)it may often be the main feature. As Ralph Waldo Emerson, the nineteenth-century American philosopher, said, 'It is very certain that each man carries in his eye the exact indication of his rank in the immense scale of men, and we are always learning to read (5)it.' Indeed, psychological experiments suggest that we make judgements of each other's social status within the first few seconds of meeting. No wonder first impressions count, and no wonder we feel social evaluation anxieties!

35

40

1 本文に即して、下線部（1）の具体的な内容を 100 字以内の日本語（句読点を含む）で説明しなさい。

10　　　　　　　　　　　　　　　　　　20　　　　　　　（一橋大）

2 下線部（2）の内容を、文脈に即して具体的に日本語で説明しなさい。　　　　（一橋大）

3 空所（3）に入れるのに最も適切な語を 1 つ選びなさい。
① anxiety ② interactions ③ commonality ④ inequality ⑤ rivalry

4 下線部（4）（5）はそれぞれ何を指すか、日本語で答えなさい。
(4)
(5)

5 本文の内容と一致するものを 2 つ選びなさい。
① Though geographical mobility rose dramatically in the last half century, people's social anxieties didn't increase as much.
② Social anxieties that today's people feel have much to do with a faceless society they live in where they don't know much about each other.
③ People today are more concerned with how others evaluate their status than with how they can interact with others.
④ People accept each other as equals in today's society too, but status differences among them have become much wider than in the nineteenth century.
⑤ In many developed countries it has become more important to measure each other's worth by their social position and social evaluation anxieties have increased.

Chapter 11

大阪大学

Newborns swaddled in a blanket are likely to cry when someone opens the blanket ⏺2-31 to expose them to the cooler temperature of the room. This cry should not be regarded as a sign of fear or anger because it is a biologically prepared reaction to the change in temperature. Moreover, genes whose products influence limbic sites⋆ are not yet active in newborns. Nor should we call a crying six-month-old who dropped her rattle *angry* because this emotion presumes knowledge of the cause of a distressed state. Charles Darwin, who kept a diary on his child, made (1)that mistake when his seven-month-old son screamed after the lemon he was playing with slipped away. The father of evolutionary theory assumed a biological continuity between animals and infants and projected the state he felt when he lost a valuable object on to both animals and his young son. Many contemporary psychologists attribute a state of fear to seven-month-olds who cry at the approach of a stranger and to forty-year-olds who notice a large amount of clotted blood in their saliva. But (2)the states of these two agents cannot be the same because of the profound biological and psychological differences between infants and adults. The infant's distress is an automatic reaction to the inability to relate the unfamiliar features of the stranger to his or her knowledge; the adult's state follows an appraisal of the meaning of the blood for his or her health.

The infant's behavioral reactions to emotional incentives are either biologically ⏺2-32 prepared responses or acquired habits, and the responses are signs of a change in internal state that is free of appraisal. The structural immaturity of the infant brain means that the emotions that require thought, such as guilt, pride, despair, shame, and empathy, cannot be experienced in the first year because the cognitive abilities necessary for their emergence have not yet developed.

The restriction on possible emotions extends beyond infancy. Children less than a ⏺2-33 year old cannot experience empathy with another or shame, whereas all three-year-olds are capable of these states because of the emergence of the ability to infer the state of others and to be conscious of one's feelings and intentions. This extremely important developmental change, due to brain maturation, adds a qualitatively new reason for actions, especially the desire to preserve a conception of self as a good person. (3)This motive, which has an emotional component, is a seminal basis for later behaviors that are called altruistic. Furthermore, children less than four years old find it difficult to retrieve the past and relate it to the present and, therefore, cannot experience the emotions of regret or nostalgia. Even preadolescents have some difficulty manipulating several representations simultaneously in working memory because of incomplete maturation of the connectivity of the dorsolateral prefrontal cortex★ to other sites. ₃₅ (4)This fact implies that seven- to ten-year-olds are protected from the emotions that emerge from a thoughtful examination of the logical inconsistency among their personal beliefs. Older adolescents, by contrast, are susceptible to the uncertainty that follows recognition of the inconsistency between their experiences and their childhood premises about sexuality, loyalty, God, or the heroic stature of their parents. The desire to repair ₄₀ the inconsistency requires some alteration in the earlier beliefs and the evocation of emotions denied to younger children. The cognitive immaturity also means that ten-year-olds are protected from arriving at the conclusion that they have explored every possible coping response to a crisis and no adaptive action is possible. As a result they cannot experience the emotion of hopelessness that can provoke a suicide attempt. ₄₅ Hence, we need to invent a vocabulary for the repertoire of states experienced by infants and young children. (5)These terms do not exist.

   ★ limbic sites「大脳辺縁系（感情・行動を司る場所）」   dorsolateral prefrontal cortex「側背前頭前皮質」

1 下線部（1）that mistake の意味内容を日本語で簡潔に説明しなさい。　　　　　　　（大阪大）

------

2 下線部（2）に関し、二者の状態の違いを、本文の内容に即して日本語で説明しなさい。

------

3 下線部（3）の意味内容を日本語で簡潔に説明しなさい。　　　　　　　　　　　（大阪大）

------

4 下線部（4）を日本語に直しなさい。

次ページへ続く→

5 下線部（5）の意味内容を日本語で簡潔に説明しなさい。 （大阪大）

....

6 本文の内容と一致するものを2つ選びなさい。

① If a newborn baby cries when he is suddenly exposed to the cooler temperature, it is because of his prepared biological reaction to the change in temperature.

② If a seven-month-old cries when a stranger approaches her, it is because she relates the features of the stranger to those of someone she knows.

③ A child less than a year old cannot experience empathy or shame because the cognitive abilities necessary for their emergence have not yet developed.

④ Children more than one year old can experience the emotion of nostalgia because they can relate the past to the present.

⑤ Children between seven and ten years old are easily affected by emotions which emerge from the logical inconsistency among their personal beliefs.

Memo

Chapter 12

What is the natural human diet? For centuries, people have been debating the best ⏎2-38 foods, often making it a question of the morality of eating other animals. (1)The lion has no choice, but we do. A lot of vegetarians say we should not eat meat.

But while humans don't have the sharp teeth to kill and eat other animals, that ⏎2-39
5 doesn't mean we aren't "supposed" to eat meat. Our early human ancestors invented weapons and cutting tools to use instead of sharp meat-eating teeth.

And gluten isn't unnatural either. (2)Despite the widespread call to cut ⏎2-40 carbohydrates★, there's plenty of evidence that cereal grains were basic foods, at least for some, long before they were planted. People in the present-day area of Iraq ate
10 several grains during the peak of the last ice age, more than 10,000 years before these grains were planted. There's nothing new about cereal consumption.

This leads us to the Paleolithic★ diet. As a paleoanthropologist★, I'm often asked ⏎2-41 for my thoughts about it. I'm not really a fan — I like pizza and French fries and ice cream too much. Nevertheless, (3)diet experts have built a strong case for the differences
15 between what we eat today and what our ancestors evolved to eat. The idea is that our diets have changed too quickly for our genes to keep up; the result is said to be metabolic syndrome, a group of conditions including high blood pressure, high blood-sugar levels, high cholesterol levels, and being overweight.

Paleolithic diets make sense, and it's no surprise that they remain hugely popular. ⏎2-42
20 There are many variants on the general theme, but foods rich in protein and fatty acids show up again and again. Meat from grass-fed cows and fish are good, and carbohydrates should come from fresh fruits and vegetables. On the other hand, cereal grains, dairy, potatoes, and highly refined and processed foods are out. The idea is to eat like our Stone Age ancestors.

25 I am not a food expert, and cannot speak with authority about the nutritional costs ⏎2-43 and benefits of Paleolithic diets, but I can comment on our evolutionary beginnings. From the standpoint of paleoecology★, the Paleolithic diet is a myth. Food choice is as much about what's available to be eaten as it is about what a species evolved to eat. And just as fruits ripen, leaves change colors, and flowers bloom predictably at different
30 times of the year, foods available to our ancestors varied over time as the world changed around them from warm and wet to cool and dry and back again. Those changes are what drove our evolution.

Many paleoanthropologists today believe that increasingly unstable climates through the Pleistocene★ helped our ancestors to develop a flexibility toward various diets, which has become a key characteristic of humanity. The basic idea is that our ever-changing world has eliminated most of the choosey eaters among us. (4)<u>Nature has made us an adaptable species.</u> Thus, we have been able to change from food gatherers to farmers, and have really begun to consume our planet. ₃₅

★ carbohydrates「炭水化物」 Paleolithic「旧石器時代の」 paleoanthropologist「古人類学者」 paleoecology「古生態学」 Pleistocene「更新世」

1 下線部（1）の意味を、本文の内容に即して日本語で簡潔に説明しなさい。

....
....

2 下線部（2）を日本語に直しなさい。

....
....

3 下線部（3）の人たちの考え方を、本文の内容に即して日本語で簡潔に説明しなさい。

....
....

4 筆者は食べ物の選択についてどのように考えているか。本文中からその考えを最も端的に述べた1文を探し、その意味を日本語で説明しなさい。

....
....

5 下線部（4）の意味を、最終段落の内容に即して日本語で簡潔に説明しなさい。

....
....

6 本文の内容と一致するものを2つ選びなさい。

① The ancient people in today's Iraq started to eat cereal grains after they succeeded in planting and harvesting them for consumption.

② Many diet experts propose that people go back to the Paleolithic diet because it was rich in protein and carbohydrates.

③ The author thinks from the standpoint of paleoecology that because our world was ever changing, the diet of our ancestors was also changing.

④ Though the author is not a food expert, he argues that in food choice evolution plays a more important role than what is available to be eaten.

⑤ Many paleoanthropologists today believe that our ancestors developed the dietary flexibility in the face of climatic variations.

One of the best measures for judging the true complexity of a job is how easily it can ◉2-49 be replaced by a machine. In the early days of the automation revolution, most people thought that technology would cause jobs to disappear from the bottom up. The factory, it seemed, would be the place this reduction would happen first. (1)<u>Assembly-line workers</u> tightening the same few bolts would be swept away by machines doing the job faster, more efficiently and without complaint. (2)<u>Mid-level supervisors</u> would fare better, since no robot would be able to manage the remaining workforce. Fewer manual laborers, however, would mean the loss of at least some managers. It would only be at (3)<u>the top ranks of the organization</u> that jobs would be safe from machines.

To a degree that happened. Robots did replace many bolt-turners, but the losses ◉2-50 went only so far. No machine could bring the multiple senses to the job that a human can, feeling the way a car door just doesn't click properly in its frame or noticing a small flaw in a half-finished product. Robots might perform truly automatic, repetitive tasks, but jobs that required complex human skills and the ability to think independently were safe.

Meanwhile, one level above the manual workers, the mid-level management jobs ◉2-51 started to vanish, as employees required less direct instruction. However, at the top of the ladder, the bosses and executives, whose jobs often called for subtle anticipation of markets and expert reactions to changing demands and trends, did, for the most part, keep their positions.

The computer revolution had even greater impact on the workforce by automating ◉2-52 the handling of information. This caused the mid-level job loss that started in the factory to [　A　]. While such a development may have caught a lot of hard-working employees by surprise, it was in fact a very predictable result.

The vast range of jobs and professions follows a U-shaped complexity curve. At its ◉2-53 left peak are the bluest of the blue-collar jobs, the ones often held in the least esteem and usually the most poorly paid. At the right peak are the whitest of the white-collar jobs — very highly regarded and equally highly paid. Most people, however, work in the middle — in the valley of the U — where the jobs are the simplest.

Nothing better illustrates how the complexity U-curve works than airline ticketing ◉2-54 clerks, low-status workers once thought likely to be replaced by automated kiosks. The next time you're in an airport, you will see just as many clerks as there ever were. While a kiosk might be fine for the individual traveler with a single suitcase, it's no good at all to a disabled passenger who needs help boarding a plane, or to anxious parents trying to arrange care for a young child flying alone. Often, human assistance is the only way to solve a problem, particularly if it requires a little creativity or includes an emotional aspect that calls for a personal touch.

2-55　　The jobs at the other end of the U-curve [　　B　　]. It's here that you find the lawyer reading through documents to construct a legal argument; the biochemist gathering test results and making an intuitive leap that leads to a new cure; the psychologist responding to facial, vocal and physical gestures that reveal more than words can.

2-56　　It's only in the lower parts of the complexity U-curve that things are a bit simpler. There, the jobs most often [　　C　　]. (4)In industrialized parts of the world, the growing ability of computers to do this kind of work has led to a hollowing-out of the workforce, with many office clerks and bookkeepers losing their jobs.

1　下線部（1）～（3）の職種について、a：自動化革命初期に工場で起こると予想されたこと、b：実際に起きたこと、をそれぞれ本文に即して日本語で簡潔に説明しなさい。句読点も含め25字以内であること。

(1) a
(1) b

(2) a
(2) b

(3) a
(3) b

2　本文に関する次の質問に、日本語で簡潔に答えなさい。

Why were airline ticketing clerks not replaced by automated kiosks when the machines were introduced in airports?

3　下線部（4）を日本語に直しなさい。

次ページへ続く→

4 　[A] ～ [C] に入れるのに最も適切なものをそれぞれ１つずつ選びなさい。ただし、同じ番号を複数回用いてはならない。

（東京大・改）

① 　involve collecting and transmitting information

② 　provide secure foundations for future prosperity

③ 　spread to office tasks like evaluating loan applications

④ 　determine what we can take of value from our experiences

⑤ 　rely even more heavily on intellectual and instinctive skills

5 　本文の内容と一致するものを１つ選びなさい。

① 　The reason for the loss of mid-level management jobs after the automation revolution was that employees did not need as much direct instruction as before.

② 　The computer revolution, which surprised a lot of hard-working employees, didn't have as much impact on the workforce as the automation revolution.

③ 　You can tell from the U-shaped complexity curve that the simplest jobs are done mostly by the blue-collar workers.

④ 　The U-shaped increase in air travelers was one reason why airline ticketing clerks were not taken over by automated kiosks.

Memo

Chapter 14

The most common conception of deserts and arid lands, as embodied by the 1994 🔊 2-61 UN Convention to Combat Desertification, innumerable national development agencies, and many nongovernmental organizations, is that they are barren, deforested, overgrazed lands — wastelands with little value that need to be repaired and improved. Up to 70% of global arid and semiarid lands are frequently claimed to be suffering from varying degrees of desertification. (1)Yet the word "desertification" has no agreed definition, measures of desertification are not standardized, and it is very difficult to differentiate degradation caused by humans from the effects of drought in the drylands, which makes such estimates of desertification questionable at best. Indeed, academic research has shown for more than 25 years that estimates of desertification have been significantly exaggerated and that most of the world's drylands are not being invaded by spreading deserts caused by deforestation, burning, and overgrazing as claimed since the word was first invented nearly one hundred years ago. This has led a majority of arid lands ecologists to conclude that there is insufficient scientific evidence of large-scale permanent desertification.

Desertification as a concept is extremely important, however, not least because the 🔊 2-62 fear it generates drives a multimillion-dollar global anti-desertification campaign that impacts the lives of millions of people. Desertification is also important because it was the first major environmental issue to be recognized as occurring on a global scale. (2)As such, the way that the "crisis of desertification" was conceptualized, framed, and tackled as a policy problem shaped in numerous ways our reactions to subsequent environmental crises such as deforestation, biodiversity loss, and climate change. Global concern about desertification is most commonly dated to the 1970s when a great drought and famine hit the sub-Saharan region with terrible suffering and mortality, and resulted in coordinated global action in the form of the 1977 UN Conference on Desertification. Fear of desertification, though, has driven global dryland policy for much longer, dating to the mid-twentieth century with UNESCO's Arid Zone Program and to various colonial adventures in the world's drylands long before that.

Indeed, before the word "desertification" was invented in the 1920s by a French 🔊 2-63 colonial forester, western imperial powers had executed many different programs to try to restrain the perceived spread of desert regions and also to try to "restore" the drylands to productivity according to capitalist goals. Underlying these attempts was a complex, long-standing, and primarily Anglo-European understanding of deserts which equated them with ruined forests much of the time. (3)Examining how these ideas about deserts have changed over the long duration will reveal that many of the worst 35 cases of degradation in the drylands have been the result of policies based on the old ideas that deserts are without value and that desertification is caused primarily by "traditional" uses of the land by local populations. Societies in arid lands have, in fact, lived successfully in these unpredictable environments for thousands of years using ingenious techniques. (4)The assumption that the world's drylands are worthless and 40 deforested landscapes has led, since the colonial period, to programs and policies that have often systematically damaged dryland environments and marginalized large numbers of indigenous peoples, many of whom had been using the land sustainably.

■ 下線部（1）を、"such estimates" の指す内容が具体的にわかるように日本語に直しなさい。 （京都大・改）

② 下線部（2）を、"As such" の指す内容が具体的にわかるように日本語に直しなさい。 （京都大）

③ 下線部（3）を日本語に直しなさい。

④ 下線部（4）を日本語に直しなさい。 （京都大）

Memo

Memo

Memo

Memo

Chapter 1

テーマ解説

　機械工学や医学と比較すると、動物の研究はその意義がわかりにくいと感じる人も多いだろう。その目的はさまざまだが、その中でも**生体模倣技術 (biomimetics)** は急速に発展している科学分野の1つである。

　その一例が、ハエの目の構造が、**太陽電池（solar cell）**のエネルギー効率を高める技術の発展に貢献したことである。ある科学者が、ハエの目に微細な筋があり、その溝の凹凸が連続していることを発見した。その科学者は、ハエの目の模型を作り、光がどのように反射するかを調べた。すると、溝の凹凸が光が通過するのを促進していることがわかった。つまり、ハエの目は、弱い光の中でも見ることができるように、四方からくる光を吸収することが可能だったのである。その後、現代の素材を使ってハエの目の構造を模した装置を作り、それを太陽光パネルに取り付けると、従来のものに比べてエネルギー受容率が10%増加した。今もこのハエの目の構造は、特定の集光装置の設計基準になっている。

▶ **本文出典**

　アメリカの雑誌 *Science* のウェブサイト上で 2017 年 7 月 17 日に公開された、Sid Perkins 氏による記事 Why midsized animals are the fastest on Earth の一部を抜粋したもの。

　本書では、問題作成のため、入試問題本文から一部省略している。

▶ **muscle cells**

　筋細胞。一つ一つが細長い繊維状になっているため、筋繊維（線維）（muscle fibers）とも呼ばれる。これらが束になったものを筋束（muscle fascicle）、さらにこれが集合したものが筋肉組織（muscle tissue）となり、いわゆる筋肉となる。

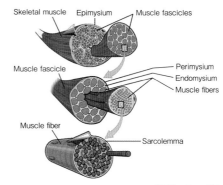

骨格筋のイメージ図

▶ **ectotherms**

　外温動物。外部の温度によって体温が変化する動物のこと。主に爬虫類、魚類、昆虫等がこれに該当する。

▶ **endotherms**

　内温動物。外部の温度にかかわらず、自分の体温をある程度一定に保つことができる動物のこと。哺乳類や鳥類が該当する。

▶ **"fast-twitch" muscle fibers**

　速筋繊維。骨格筋のうち、素早く収縮し、瞬間的に大きな力を出すことができるもの。白っぽい色合いをしているため白筋繊維とも呼ばれる。

▶ **"slow-twitch" fibers**

　遅筋繊維。速筋細胞に比べると収縮スピードが遅く、瞬間的な力を出すことはできない。その代わりに持久力が高く、長時間一定の筋力を維持することができる。赤い色合いをしているため赤筋繊維とも呼ばれる。

Chapter 2

テーマ解説

　我々はしばしば「有史以来」という言葉を使う。この**有史（recorded history）**とは、記録された言語、すなわち「文字」の現存をもって定義されている。もちろん、有史より前にも人々の生活はあったはずだ。しかし、文字という記録媒体が残っていないために、彼らがどのような**知識（knowledge）・知恵（wisdom）**をもって生活をしていたのかを、現代の私たちには正しく知ることができない。口承、すなわち記録されない言語によって伝えられた知識・知恵は、その語り部がいなくなれば伝承の手段を永久に失い、消失することになる。それがいかに優れた知識・知恵であっても、文字として残っていなければ、現代を生きる私たちにとって「存在しなかった」も同然である。

　たとえ文字として記録されていても、時がたつにつれて読める人がいなくなるというのもよくあることだ。古代エジプトのヒエログリフは、エジプト人によってではなく、19世紀のフランス人によって解読された。文字が残っていても、その内容を正しく後世に伝えていくことが容易でないのは、古文を学習する皆さんも実感するところだろう。

▶ **本文出典**

　アメリカの雑誌 *Whole Earth Catalogue* の 2000 年春号に掲載された、Rosemarie Ostler 氏による記事 Disappering Languages の冒頭を抜粋したもの。

▶ **Michael Krauss**

　1934-。アメリカの言語学者。1991 年のアメリカ言語学会において初めて、危機に瀕する言語の世界的な問題を提起した。2000 年にアラスカ先住民言語センター所長を引退した後も、この問題に精力的に取り組んでいる。

▶ **Stephen Wurm**

　1922-2001。ハンガリー生まれの言語学者。1957 年にオーストラリア国籍を取得し、同地先住民の多くの言葉を研究した。

Chapter 3

　エッセイ（essay） は、筆者が耳にしたり経験したりした出来事から自分自身で何かを考え、その考えを読者に伝えたいという意図があって書かれるものだ。ほとんどの場合一人称の視点で表現され、物語と違って筆者の考え方が直接的に示されることも多い。論理的な展開は論説文ほど厳密でないこともあるが、科学的な内容であれ、人生訓めいた内容であれ、あるいは何気ない日常の一風景であれ、「筆者が読者に何を伝えたいと思っているか」をしっかりと把握することが大切だ。伝えたいことは事件や事柄自体ではない。それを通じて筆者が考えたことを伝えたいのである。

　本文とは異なるが、入試に出題される英文のエッセイには人生訓めいた内容のものが多くある。筆者が見聞きする出来事はそれこそ無限にあるが、そこからたどり着く主旨は **「よりよい生活に導こうとする」** ものに集約されることがほとんどだ。かつて筆者が持っていた傾向が、ある出来事を見聞きすることによって新たな傾向を手に入れ、それによって生活がよりよい方向に向かったとき、筆者はその経験を読者に伝えたいと思うのだ。「こうしなさい」という直接的な表現がなくても、**筆者は行間に必ずその意図を込めている。**

▶ 本文出典

　アメリカの雑誌 *Newsweek* のオンライン版に 2000 年 3 月掲載された Shoba Narayan 氏によるエッセイ "A sari for a month" を一部変更したもの。

▶ sari

　インドやバングラデシュ、パキスタンなど南アジアの女性が着用する民族衣装。インドでは近代化に伴って女性の衣装も西洋化しつつあり、デリーやカルカッタなどの大都市部での着用率は 3 割以下になっている。

▶ Hindus

　ヒンドゥー教。インド、ネパールを中心に全世界で約 9 億人の信者を持つ宗教。キリスト教や仏教と異なり、開祖によって始まった宗教ではなく、習慣や社会制度、価値観などを共有する地域ごとの民間信仰を起源とする。それゆえに統一化された信仰形態はなく、多神教である。

　不殺生を教義とするため、ヒンドゥー教徒の多くは菜食主義者だが、鶏卵や鶏肉を口にする人も一定数存在する。

▶ Marilyn Monroe's dress

　1957 年の映画『七年目の浮気』（The Seven Year Itch）の中で、主人公を演じた米国の女優マリリン・モンロー（Marilyn Monroe, 1926-1962）が着用していた白いドレスのこと。地下鉄の通気口から吹き出す風で白いドレスがまくれ上がるシーンは、ハリウッド映画を最も象徴するシーンとして有名。

Chapter 4

テーマ解説

　自然科学系の入試長文では、**地球温暖化（global warming）** と比肩する頻度で、動物の特徴が扱われる。2011 年度だけを見ても、**ミツバチ（honeybee）** の生態・情報伝達（大阪工業大・南山大・武蔵大）、**チンパンジー（chimpanzee）** や **ゴリラ（gorilla）** など霊長類の行動（東邦大・明治大・広島修道大・文教大・北里大・順天堂大・京都外国語大）、**イルカ（dolphin）** を代表とする動物同士のコミュニケーション・文化（名古屋学院大・高崎経済大・関西大）、**小型ほ乳類（small mammal）** や **げっ歯類（rodent）** の **適者生存（the survival of the fittest）** 能力（神戸大・センター試験）、**バクテリア（bacteria）** や **菌類（fungi）** に支えられた **生態系（ecosystem）**（成城大・東京医科大・帯広畜産大・北九州市立大・奈良県立医科大・山形大）など、枚挙にいとまがない。

　論調は、森林や海洋などの自然環境が持つ **生物多様性（biodiversity）** が人間の活動によって破壊され、**種の絶滅（extinction of species）** の危機に追いやられる—というものが多いが、他にも、犬と人との関係の歴史（法政大）、**気候変動（climate change）** による動植物の **適応（adaptation）**（信州大）、環境保護を目的とした観光 **エコツーリズム（eco-tourism）**（立命館大）など、視点や切り口はさまざまである。

▶ 本文出典

Colin Tudge, *The Bird: A Natural History of Who Birds are, Where They Came From and How They Live,* Crown, 2009.

　コリン・タッジ氏（1943-）は英国の科学作家。動植物全般の著作があり、ユーモアに富む筆致に定評がある。

▶ homing pigeon

©Andreas Trepte

carrier pigeon とも言う。日本語で伝書バトだが、近年はその役割の変化から、レース鳩と呼ばれることもある。

伝書バト

▶ ammonia

窒化物の 1 つで、分子式は NH_3。生物の代謝活動などで生成され、尿などによって体外に排出される。刺激臭がある。

▶ radio

　無線通信のこと。イギリス政府の支援を受けた、イタリア人のグリエルモ・マルコーニが世界で初めて無線通信に成功したのは 1895 年のこと。実際に船舶や海軍で利用されるようになったのは 20 世紀に入ってからと考えられる。

▶ telescope

　ここでは sextant「六分儀」のこと。天測航法時に、天体高度や測定対象の位置の割り出しに用いられる。

六分儀

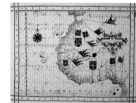

16 世紀の西アフリカの海図

▶ chart

　ここでは nautical chart「海図」のこと。15 世紀の大航海時代以降、探索・侵略・交流を目的とした航海には必須かつ貴重なものだった。

▶ table

　一般的にはデータベース等の「表」のことだが、ここでは天体の日時ごとの位置を表にしたものを指す。現在は nautical almanac「航海年鑑、天測暦」などと呼ばれ、日本では毎年海上保安庁より出版されている。

▶ Orion

　オリオン座（発音は［オライオン］）。リゲル、ベテルギウスを含む、北半球では代表的な冬の星座の 1 つ。天の赤道上にあるので南半球でも見ることができる。多くの国で神話の素材となっており、ギリシア神話では海神ポセイドンを父に持つ巨大なハンターとして描かれる。

▶ Taurus

　牡牛座。星占いで有名な黄道十二星座の 1 つで、オリオン座に隣接している。ギリシア神話では主神ゼウスの化身とされ、後の「ヨーロッパ」の語源となる女性エウロパを背に乗せて、地中海の海面をクレタ島まで駆け抜けたという神話が残る。

▶ North Star

　北極星。polar star や Polaris とも表現される。こぐま座を構成する星の 1 つ（α星）。北斗七星やカシオペア座を利用して位置を知ることができる。

Chapter 5

テーマ解説

　貧困国の子どもたちにとって「学ぶ理由」は明確である。学ぶことによって身につける学力やスキルは、彼らが大人になったときの生活能力に直結する。彼らにとって学ぶことは生きることと同じで、より学ぶことは将来のより豊かな暮らしを意味する。

　しかし、それを熱望したからといって容易に手に入れられるほど彼らの環境は甘くない。不安定な**政情（political situation）**や**雇用（employment）**、それに伴う**苦しい家計（financial hardship / tight budget）**によって、子どもたちは働かざるを得ず、将来のための学ぶ機会を奪われる。学びたいのに学べない、貧しい今日を生き残るために将来の豊かな暮らしを捨てざるを得ない、そして貧しさから抜け出せない―この悪循環はまさに悲劇というほかはない。

　日本国憲法が、「教育を受けさせる義務」と「教育を受ける権利」を規定し、わたしたちがとくに疑問を持たずにその権利を行使できていることは幸いである。将来の豊かな生活のために、存分に学ぶことができるのだから。

▶ OECD

　経済協力開発機構。本部はフランスのパリ。欧州を中心とした先進 30 カ国間の自由な意見・情報の交換を通じて、経済成長、貿易の自由化、途上国支援に貢献することを目的とする団体。

▶ sub-Saharan Africa

　アラブ系住民が多い地中海に面する北アフリカ諸国に対し、黒人が多いサハラ砂漠以南の地域・国家を表す。一般的に、アフリカ諸国の貧困、政治の腐敗、治安の悪さ、エイズの蔓延などは、この地域において顕著とされる。

▶ Mali and Mozanbique

　いずれもサハラ砂漠以南に位置するアフリカ国家。

　マリ共和国は 1960 年にフランスから独立した後、複数のクーデターを経て共和制を敷くに至った。比較的政情は安定している。

　モザンビーク共和国では、1975 年にポルトガルから独立した後、長く内戦が続いたが、終結後は比較的順調な経済成長を続けている。HIV の問題解決が急務。

▶ South and West Asia

　南アジアはインドを中心とした 7 〜 9 カ国を表す。西アジアはいわゆる中東のことで、地中海の東側にあるおよそ20 カ国を指す。

▶ last primary grade

　小学校（primary school）での最終学年（日本では 6 年生）のこと。

▶ 本文出典

　UNESCO による、万人のための教育（Education for All; EFA）プロジェクトの 2009 年報告書、*Global Monitoring Report for 2009* の一部を調整したもの。

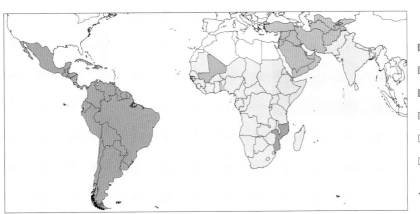

　　■ Latin America

　　■ Republic of Mali

　　■ Republic of Mozambique

　　■ West Asian countries

　　□ South Asian countries

　　□ sub-Saharan
　　　 African countries

＊ただし、構成国家は定義によって異なることがある。

Chapter 6

テーマ解説

　研究する対象が同じでも、そのアプローチを変えることによって見え方が全く異なってくることがある。文学評論家の江藤淳は、大学時代に著した論文「夏目漱石」、後年の『漱石とその時代』によって、文豪として半ば神格化されていた世間の漱石像を一変させた。漱石もまたある一面においては人間関係や体調に悩む市井の人と変わらないことを明らかにし、その結果、かつてのものとは異なる新たな魅力を漱石の作品群に与えることになった。同氏の解釈手法は、賛否はさておき、文学研究における革新だったと言えるかもしれない。

　同様の革新的な解釈や新手法は、科学、史学などさまざまな分野で確認されている。当然のものとされてきた従来の考え方や価値観が、あるきっかけで劇的に変化することを**パラダイムシフト（paradigm shift）**と呼ぶことがあるが、誰も試みたことのないアプローチから結ばれる新たな像は、驚きを伴って私たちの視野を広げてくれる。

▶ 本文出典

Tim Harford, *The Logic of Life: The Rational Economics of an Irrational World*, Random House, 2008.

▶ Abraham Darby

　エイブラハム・ダービー1世（1678-1717）を指す。ダービー家は3代にわたって、コールブルックデールの鋳造工場で鉄製品を作り続けた。1世の孫であるエイブラハム・ダービー3世（1750-1791）は、1780年に世界初の鉄橋であるコールブルックデール橋（別名 The Iron Bridge）を建設した。これは世界遺産に登録されており、産業革命の象徴的建造物と見なされることがある。

コールブルックデール橋

▶ Robert C. Allen

　1947-。オックスフォード大学の経済学史教授。この文章は、同教授による論文 *The British Industrial Revolution in Global Perspective: How Commerce Created The Industrial Revolution and Modern Economic Growth*（2006）に取材しているところが大きい。ちなみに、筆者の Tim Harford もオックスフォード大学の出身である。

▶ spinning jenny

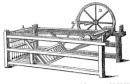

　18世紀中頃、イギリスのジェームズ・ハーグリーブスが発明したとされる紡績機。

ジェニー紡績機

▶ water frame

　18世紀中頃、イギリスのアークライトが発明した水力紡績機。ジェニー紡績機よりも丈夫な糸を紡ぐことができる改良版として位置づけられている。

Chris55

水力紡績機

▶ steam engine

　蒸気機関。産業革命を強力に推進した革新的技術として、スコットランドのジェームズ・ワットによる発明が代表的である。

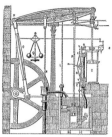

ボールトンとワットの蒸気機関

Chapter 7

テーマ解説

　グーグルは、携帯電話やタブレット等の端末の初期設定に、自社の検索サービスを採用させることを重視している。それを最も顕著に証明する例は、グーグルがアップルに2021年だけで約1兆6,500億円以上を支払ったことだ。グーグルの検索エンジンをアップルのiPhoneやiPad等における検索機能の**初期設定（default）**とすることへの対価として、検索広告収入の一部をアップルに分配したのである。グーグルは2016年に自社の検索エンジンの利用回数が全世界で年間約2兆回あったと公表しているが、その約半数がアップル製端末からのものだった。

　米国司法省は2020年10月、**反トラスト法［独占禁止法］（antitrust law）**に抵触するとしてグーグルを提訴した。グーグルの検索サービスは全世界で約90%という驚異的な**市場占有率（market share）**を誇る。司法省は、その高い占有率を獲得し維持する手法が、自由な競争環境と消費者の利益を阻害していると考えている。司法省が問題視していることの1つは、グーグル社が端末メーカーに求めた「協定」である。グーグルは、アップル製端末以外で広く利用されている自社OSのアンドロイドを採用する際、初期設定である自社の検索アプリやブラウザを削除しないよう求め、同意しない場合、OSだけでなくYouTubeや地図、メール等の主要サービスの利用を認めていない。

　一方、グーグルは「利用者が他社の検索機能を利用することは可能であり、グーグルの利用を強制されていない。さらに検索は無料であり、利用者の利益を害することはしていない」と反論している。かつて、ウィンドウズOSで市場を席巻したマイクロソフトは司法省に提訴されたが、その後10年以上をその訴訟に費やし、その間にIT企業の主役の座をグーグルやアップルに奪われた。現在、圧倒的な市場占有率を誇るグーグルの最大の敵は、一企業の独占を嫌う国家なのかもしれない。

▶ the Holy Grail

　聖杯。イエス・キリストが最後の晩餐で葡萄酒を飲むときに用いた杯。またこの杯は、イエス・キリストが十字架に磔にされた際に流した血を受けたものと同一とされている。

　中世ヨーロッパでは、聖杯を探し求める物語である「聖杯伝説」が数多く作られた。それらの多くは騎士の武者修行の様子を描いた騎士道文学だった。典型的なストーリーは、聖杯探求の使命を負った騎士が見知らぬ土地を冒険し、ドラゴンや巨人といった想像上の怪物との対決などの数々の試練を乗り越えながら聖杯を得て、王に認められるというものであった。こうした物語から、the Holy Grail は本文（注）にあるような「熱心に追い求めるもの」、あるいは「究極の目標」という意味でも使われるようになった。

▶ fair game

　（批判、嘲笑、攻撃などの）かっこうの的、カモ。または法的に狩猟が許可されている鳥獣。game には「遊戯、競技」といった意味のほか、「狩猟時の獲物、またその肉」という意味がある。

　fair は「公正な、公平な」という意味を持つので、「公正な試合」と訳されることもある（*ex.* Let's play a fair game!「公正な試合をしよう」）。

Chapter 8

▶ **本文出典**

　Tor Nørretranders, *2014 :WHAT SCIENTIFIC IDEA IS READY FOR RETIREMENT?* という英文記事を一部改変したもの。筆者は、デンマークの作家、思想家。

▶ **Auguste Comte**

　1798-1857。フランスの哲学者、社会学者、数学者。実証主義哲学を提唱し、社会学 (sociology) という言葉を造った人物。人間の思考や知性は、神学的段階、形而上学的段階、実証的段階の3つの段階を経て発展するという、「三段階の法則」を主張した。代表著作は、『実証哲学講義』（全6巻、1830-42年）

▶ **behavioral science**

　行動科学。人間の行動を客観的に観察、分析し、そこから一定の法則を科学的に導こうとする学問。1950年前後からアメリカを中心に発展し、主に心理学、社会学、人類学、精神医学などがこれに含まれる。消費者心理を分析するマーケティング活動や、人材育成における目標管理など、さまざまな場面で応用されている。

▶ **neurobiology**

　神経生物学。神経科学（neuroscience）とも。神経細胞や神経組織などの神経系に関する研究を科学的に行う学問。その研究範囲は非常に広く、神経構造や神経機能などの分子レベルの分析だけでなく、学習や行動、認知メカニズムの解明なども対象としている。

▶ **prosocial behavior**

　向社会的行動。向社会的（prosocial）とは、反社会的・非社会的の対義語にあたるもの。向社会的行動とは、他人を助けることや他人に対して積極的な態度を示すことなどを、自発的に行うことである。

Chapter 9

テーマ解説

　現代における**科学（science）**とは、客観的事象を集め、それを調査し、原因と結果を求めるものである。**客観的（objectivization）**でありかつ論理的なものであり、結果に対する何かしらの意図は許されない。一般的に、ある理論が科学であるか否かは、それが**科学的手法（scientific method）**に依っているか否か、すなわち仮説と理論があり、証拠に依拠していて、誰にでも再現可能なものであるかどうか、つまり実証性と再現性の条件を満たしているか否かで判断される。一方、それを満たさないもの、例えば消費者をだますために創造された（科学を装った）理論や、不正行為を根拠とした理論などは**疑似科学（pseudoscience）**と呼ばれる。

　歴史の中で、科学が大きな力を得るようになったのは、実質的に**天動説（Geocentrism）**が破棄された17世紀の**科学革命（Scientific Revolution）**以降である。それ以前の自然現象に関する探求は、哲学や思想、宗教との境界線が曖昧な思索的なもので、実証性や再現性は重んじられていなかった。しかし、**地動説（Heliocentrism）**を唱えたガリレオ・ガリレイは、自説を証明するための実験方法を公開し、再現作業を広く促すという、現代の科学的手法に通じる手法を用いて実証性と再現性を担保した。キリスト教の教義に反するにもかかわらず地動説が徐々に認知されていったのは、天動説に比べて惑星の動きを正確に計算できるからだったが、これは実証性が強い説得力を持っていることの証と言える。「科学」という概念が生まれたのは18世紀のことだが、17世紀のこうした動きが「科学的な考え方」の基礎になったのである。

▶ **本文出典**

　Chad Orzel, *Eureka! Discovering Your Inner Scientist*, Basic Books, 2014. を一部抜粋、一部改変したもの。

Chapter 10

テーマ解説

社会（society）とは、人々が集まって組織し、共同生活をする集団のことで、家族から国家まで大小さまざまな単位がある。社会が変化すれば、そこでの生活や考え方、価値観も変化する。例えば日本における家族という社会集団を見たとき、かつては「家制度」という先祖から引き継がれる血縁集団の概念があり、三世代以上が一つの家屋に居住する「大家族」もよく見受けられた。現在は「夫婦とその子ども」以下の構成員による「核家族」（一般的に単身世帯は含まない）がより一般的となり、その結果、子どもの孤独や近所関係の希薄化、高齢者単身世帯の増加などが、新たな問題として取り上げられているところである。

プライバシーを守ることと他者に無関心であることは、ともすると表裏一体である。他者との強い結びつきの中で生活していれば、自分自身の社会的な位置を確認しやすい一方、それによってプライバシーが損なわれる可能性がある。逆に、他者とかかわらずに生活していれば、プライバシーは守られても、自分自身と他者との相対的な位置が理解できず、社会に対する不安は増大する。不安な社会の中で**自己（self）**を確立するために、孤独に自分自身と向き合う人々は少なくない。

▶ **本文出典**

Richard Wilkinson and Kate Pickett, *The Spirit Level: Why Greater Equality Makes Societies Stronger*, Penguin Group, 2009.
邦訳『平等社会―経済成長に代わる、次の目標』は、2010 年に東洋経済新報社から出版されている。

▶ **social evaluative threat**

カリフォルニア大学心理社会行動学部准教授の Sally S. Dickerson 氏は、次のように説明している。a context in which the self can be judged negatively by others「自己が他者から否定的に評価されうる状況」。

Chapter 11

テーマ解説

認知科学を含む脳研究は、活発であるがゆえに異説も多い。ここでは一般的と考えられる説を、理解のしやすさを主眼に解説する。

脳（brain）は大きく分けて、大脳・小脳・脳幹に分類されるが、社会生活において重要視されるのは大脳の働きである。とくに**前頭前皮質（prefrontal cortex）**（日本語の呼称はさまざまだが、大脳新皮質と呼ばれる大脳表層の、前方部分と覚えておけばよいだろう）は、情報を統合・操作する司令塔的役割を担い、集中力、感情・行動の制御、コミュニケーション力、決断力などを主に司るとされる。

記憶には、**短期記憶（short-term memory）**と**長期記憶（long-term memory）**の２つがあるとされる。五感による**知覚情報（sensory information）**は、**大脳辺縁系（limbic system）**（大脳新皮質に囲まれた内側の、脳幹を取り囲む部分）の一部である**海馬（hippocampus）**に送られ、一時的に保存される短期記憶となる。海馬は短期記憶のうち重要度の高い記憶を大脳新皮質（主に側頭葉）に送り、長期記憶として保存する。近年とくに研究が盛んな**作業記憶（working memory）**は、短期記憶の一種とされることが多いが、脳の活動部位には諸説がある。状況に応じた、より適切な行動を選ぶために、必要な記憶を検索・選択・実行する機能を持つとされている。

▶ **本文出典**

Jerome Kagan, *What is Emotion?: History, Measures, and Meanings*, Yale University Press, 2007.
ジェローム・ケイガン（1929-）は発達心理学の先駆者と呼ばれる米国の心理学者。ハーバード大学名誉教授。

Chapter 12

テーマ解説

　現在直面している問題に対処するために、過去の経験を参考にすることに異論を唱える人はいないだろう。例えば、新型コロナウィルスの蔓延に対処するために、過去の**パンデミック (pandemic)** で蓄積された知見は、積極的に活用するべきである。

　一方、現在直面している問題に苦慮すると、その問題が存在しなかった時代の経験や様式、習慣などを高く評価する人も多い。この考え方の多くは、理性的なものではない情緒的な**懐古 (nostalgia)** であろう。現在を否定し、過去を肯定する人は時代を問わず存在していた。

　過去を高く評価することで、**逆説 (paradox)** に陥ることもある。誰の目にも明白な例は、近現代以降先進国で増加し続けている**花粉症 (hay fever)** である。花粉症が増加した理由の1つとして「清潔な環境」があると言われている。人体に有害な**細菌 (bacteria)** や**ウィルス (virus)** を避けるために、人類は公衆衛生を発展させてきた。しかしその結果、**免疫機能 (immune function)** がより敏感に働き、人体にそれほど有害ではない花粉にも反応する人が増えた。花粉症が一般的でなかった時代の衛生環境を無条件に高く評価できないことは明白である。

　人間自身の生体も、私たちを取り巻く環境も、あまりに複雑なために全てを理解することはできない。直面する問題は、それらの複雑な要素がさらに複雑に組み合わされて起こっている。前提となる「複雑な要素」が大きく異なる「過去」をそのまま適用して解決できるはずがないのである。

▶ 本文出典

　アメリカの雑誌 *Scientific American* のブログ上で 2017 年 4 月 17 日に公開された、Peter Unger 氏による記事 The "True" Human Diet を一部抜粋、一部改変したもの。

▶ vegetarians

　菜食主義者。動物の肉を避けた食事をする人々。完全に動物性食品を摂取しないわけではなく、卵や乳製品は許容する場合が多い。一方、動物性の食品一切を含まない食生活をする人々をヴィーガン (vegan) と呼ぶ。

▶ gluten

　たんぱく質の一種。小麦粉を水でこねると生成され、粘りと弾力が特徴。グルテンを摂取するとアレルギー反応が出る場合があるほか、セリアック病（体内の免疫系がグルテンに過剰反応を起こす疾患）の原因にもなる。

▶ carbohydrates

　炭水化物。たんぱく質（protein）と脂質（fat）と並んで三大栄養素とされる。炭水化物のうち糖質は活動のエネルギー源となる一方、その摂取量を制限することで減量効果がある。

▶ Paleolithic diet

　パレオダイエット。旧石器時代の食生活を真似て減量を目指す食事法。果物や野菜、ナッツ類、魚、鶏肉等、自然から比較的簡単に入手できるものを中心に食べ、穀物、豆類、乳製品、砂糖、塩、加工食品等、農耕時代以降で食べられるようになった食材を避ける。

▶ paleoanthropologist

　古人類学者。猿人から現代人類に至るまでの、ヒト科の進化過程を研究する学問。

▶ Stone Age

　石器時代。人類が石器を使用していた時代で、約200万年前に始まり、青銅器を使い始める紀元前約8000〜2000年ごろに終了する。本文ではパレオダイエットに触れていることから、ここでは我々の祖先が狩猟生活をしていた旧石器時代を意味していると思われる。

▶ paleoecology

　古生態学。化石と地層に基づいて、古代生物の生活と当時の環境との関わりを調べる学問。

▶ Pleistocene

　更新世。約258万年前から約1万1700年前までの期間で、考古学的には旧石器時代にあたる。人類はこの間に出現したとされている。世界的に気温が低く、氷河期と間氷期を数回繰り返したことが判明している。

Chapter 13

テーマ解説

　2014 年 1 月、オックスフォード大学が、2025 年までにすべての仕事の 47% が自動化される可能性があると予測する研究結果を発表した。それは主に**製造業（manufacturing）**の、しかも低賃金で働く人々の雇用を奪う可能性が最も高く、英国の全労働者の 3 人に 1 人が職を失う危険があるという。

　しかしこうした流れは今に始まったことではない。今も昔も生産活動における最大のコストは人件費だからである。1950 年代まで存在した電話交換手は交換機の自動化によって職を失った。しかし、これにはもう 1 つの側面がある。電話会社のコスト低減によって通話料は下がり、電話の**普及率（penetration）**は上昇した。これが新たな雇用を生んだことは容易に想像できる。機器の製造やインフラ整備の分野では雇用が拡大したはずである。経済学の一般的な解釈では、科学技術の進歩はほぼ例外なく雇用を奪うが、同時に経済を発展させ、それ以上の新たな雇用を生み出すのだ。しかし 2000 年代以降は、急速なグローバル化も相まって、雇用の減少と経済発展のバランスが崩れていることへの指摘が目立つのも事実だ。すなわち、**知的職業（profession）**に従事する者とそれ以外の者との間の**「格差」（rich-poor gap）**である。

　近年のこの話題の中心にあるのは **AI（artificial intelligence：人工知能）**だろう。AI が、人間では処理しきれないほど膨大な**ビッグデータ（big data）**を解析することで、自動化は不可能だと考えられてきた**外科医（surgeon）**や**金融アナリスト（financial analyst）**といった知的職業も危険になると予想され始めている。英国の理論物理学者スティーブン・ホーキング博士は「自ら能力を発展させ、加速度的に自らを再設計できる完全な AI が完成すれば、人類は終焉を迎えるだろう」と指摘している。

▶ **本文出典**

Jeffrey Kluger, *Simplexity:Why Simple Things Become Complex (and How Complex Things Can Be Made Simple)*, Hyperion, 2009.

Chapter 14

テーマ解説

悲劇 **（tragedy）** を目の当たりにしたとき、私たちはその原因が**悪意 （bad intentions）** によるもの、つまり「こうした悲劇的な状況を望んでいた悪者がどこかにいるはずだ」と考えがちである。そしてその悲劇が社会的な問題であれば、こうした人間の傾向に沿うように単純明快な「悪」を設定して報道をするマスメディアによって、その悪（とされたもの）は広く認知され、それに対する嫌悪感が社会全体で共有される。直面した悲劇的な状況に対する憤りや悲しみといった強い負の感情を沈めるためには、「悪」への嫌悪や憎しみといった強い感情が必要なのだろう。実際、愉快犯のような悪意を持った人物が引き起こす悲劇が多発している。

一方で、悪意が存在しない悲劇も無数にあることを示唆する格言がある。**「地獄への道は、善意で舗装されている （The road to hell is paved with good intentions）」**。これは一般的に「善意をもって行ったことが、悲劇的な結果を招くこと」という意味で使われる格言である。1886 年に刊行された**『資本論』 （Capital: Critique of Political Economy）** の中にこれに似た表現があることから、その著者である**カール・マルクス （Karl Marx）** による言葉だとされることが多いが、実際には諸説あって、その出自ははっきりしない。しかし少なくともヨーロッパではこの見識は古くからあったようだ。紀元前の共和制ローマ期の政治家である**カエサル（Julius Caesar）** は、「いかに悪い結果につながったとされる事例であっても、それがはじめられた当時にまで遡れば、善き意思から発していたのであった」と言ったといわれている。

▶ **本文出典**

Diana K. Davis, *The Arid Lands: History, Power, Knowledge*, The MIT Press, 2016 の第 1 章 Deserts, Dogma, and Dryland Development Policy を一部抜粋、一部改変したもの。

▶ **the UN Convention to Combat Desertification**

国際連合砂漠化対処条約。正式名称は、United Nations Convention to Combat Desertification in Those Countries Experiencing Serious Drought and/or Desertification, Particularly in Africa「深刻な干ばつ又は砂漠化に直面する国（特にアフリカの国）において砂漠化に対処するための国際連合条約」。略称は、UNCCD。1994 年 6 月 17 日、採択。2015 年時点では 194 の国と EU が締約している。正式名称の通り、本条約は、（特にアフリカ諸国を中心とする）開発途上国で深刻化している砂漠化や干ばつに対処し、それらの影響を緩和するために、国際社会が協力することを目的としている。

▶ **sub-Saharan Africa**

サハラ砂漠以南の地域。アフリカのうち、サハラ砂漠より南の地域（下図の緑色で記された地域）を指す。極度の貧困や、感染症の蔓延、食糧や飲料水の不足など、様々な問題を抱えている。

▶ **the UN Conference on Desertification**

国連砂漠化防止会議。略称は、UNCD（または、UNCOD）。ケニアのナイロビにて 1977 年に開催された。世界各地で進行する砂漠化に対処するため、各国の専門家や代表たちが集まり、砂漠化を引き起こす原因や、砂漠化がもたらすさまざまな影響を考え、その解決策について協議した。

▶ **forester**

森林官。林業、林学の専門知識を学び、森林を守り育てる森林技術者として、国有林などの管理にあたる人のこと。本文で出てくる colonial forester「植民地森林官」は、当時のフランスの森林官である André Aubréville のことで、desertification という言葉を広めた人物だとされている。

Memo

Memo

Memo

Cutting Edge
Black

定価 700 円＋税

初刷発行：2024 年 12 月 15 日

編著者：小林義昌

株式会社 エミル出版

〒102-0072　東京都千代田区飯田橋 2-8-1
TEL 03-6272-5481　FAX 03-6272-5482

ISBN978-4-86449-159-4 C7082

Cutting Edge

Black

Navi Book

Chapter 1: An elephant should ...

Chapter 3: A sari for a month ...

Chapter 4: How do migrating ...

Chapter 6: Abraham Darby ...

Chapter 11: Newborns swaddled...

Chapter 14: The most ...

ÉMILE

● 本書の使い方 ●

◆ 【語句】

　意味が空欄になっているものは、すべて入試必出の「重要語句」です。分からなければ辞書を引いて、覚えるまで何度も確認しましょう。

　音声ダウンロードを活用して、語句の正しい発音を確認しましょう。聞き流しながら語句の意味が確認できるように、音声は「英語→日本語（の意味）」の順で収録されています。

◆ 【本文解説】

　入試頻出の、少し分かりにくい構文、文構造を解説しています。難しいと感じた文については、問題を全て解いたあとでこの解説を読んで確認しましょう。また、参考書や辞書で検索しやすいように見出しをつけていますので、理解できるまで、自分で調べることが大切です。この「じっくりと読んで理解する」作業を怠ると、学習効果は半減します。粘り強く繰り返すことで、知らず知らずのうちに「読める」ようになるのです。

◆ 【段落要旨・百字要約】

　各段落ごとの要旨を完成させて、百字要約につなげる演習をします。この演習を繰り返すことで、国公立大の二次試験で問われる「要約力」「記述力」を効率的に養うことができます。

　やみくもに「書く」ことを繰り返しても、要約する力は身につきません。要約文を完成させるためには、「必要な情報と不必要な情報の選別」と「必要な情報をつなぎ合わせること」に慣れる必要があります。ここではその2点を意識しながら演習できるように構成されています。

● 目次 ●

(1)<u>An elephant should run faster than a horse — at least in theory. That's because big creatures have more of the type of muscle cells used for acceleration. Yet mid-sized animals are the fastest on Earth, a trend that researchers have long struggled to explain.</u> Now, an analysis of nearly 500 species ranging from fruit flies to whales has an answer: The muscle cells in big animals run out of fuel before the creatures can reach their theoretical maximum speed. The work may also help scientists come up with estimates for the running speeds of certain dinosaurs.

Previous studies of animal speed have focused only on certain groups of animals, such as mammals. But that premise often looks at creatures within a limited size range, says Myriam Hirt, a zoologist at the German Centre for Integrative Biodiversity Research in Leipzig. That approach may also hide underlying factors by focusing on animals that are closely related, she notes.

To get around those limitations, (2)<u>Hirt and her colleagues</u> looked at previously collected data for a wide variety of creatures, including ectotherms (so-called cold-blooded animals) as well as warm-blooded endotherms. The 474 species they considered included runners, swimmers, and flyers that ranged in weight from 30 micrograms to 100 tons.

When the scientists mapped★ a creature's top speed versus its weight, they got an inverted-U-shaped graph, with moderately sized animals on top, they report today in *Nature Ecology and Evolution*. On the largest scale, (3)<u>the trend doesn't seem to be related to biomechanics</u>, or how an animal's body parts are arranged and how its joints function, among other factors, Hirt says.

Instead, it appears to be related to a much more fundamental metabolic★ constraint: the length of time required for the animal to reach its theoretical maximum speed, based on the number of "fast-twitch★" muscle fiber cells in the creature's muscles, as compared to the length of time it takes for those cells to run out of readily available energy. ("Fast-twitch" muscle fibers contract more quickly than "slow-twitch★" fibers and generate more force more quickly, but they also fatigue more quickly.) According to the researchers' notion, (4)<u>the "fast-twitch" muscle fibers in immense creatures such as elephants and whales run out of cellular fuel long before they can reach max speed based on the overall number of such fibers.</u>

The study is also a good starting point for revealing other factors that influence a creature's maximum speed, says Christofer Clemente, an ecophysiologist at the University of the Sunshine Coast in Maroochydore, Australia, who wasn't involved in the research. One such unexplained trend is that warm-blooded land animals are usually faster than cold-blooded creatures of comparable size, whereas at sea (5)<u>the reverse</u> is usually true.

    ＊ map「マッピングする（値を座標に配置する）」 metabolic「代謝の」 fast-twitch「急激に収縮する」
       slow-twitch「ゆっくり収縮する」

1 ....

....

....

2 ....

....

....

3 （ア）..

....

（イ）It seems that the trend is related not to biomechanics but to ....

....

4 ....

....

                                    10   20

5 （空欄の解答欄）

6 ....

語句　音声は、「英語」→「日本語の意味」の順で読まれます。　CD 1- Tr 7-10

入試基礎レベル

5　fuel [fjúːəl]

11　approach [əpróutʃ]（名）

11　hide [háid]

11　factor [fǽktər]

21　arrange [əréindʒ]

22　function [fʌ́ŋkʃən]（動）

23　instead [instéd]

26　available [əvéiləbl]

32　influence [ínfluəns]（動）

入試標準レベル（共通テスト・私大）

1　in theory

2　creature [kríːtʃər]

3　struggle to *do*

4　analysis [ənǽləsis]

4　species [spíːʃiːz]

4　range from A to B

5　run out of ...

6　estimate [éstəmət]（名）

7　dinosaur [dáinəsɔ̀r]

8　previous [príːviəs]

8　focus on ...

9　limited [límitəd]

11　underlying [ʌ́ndərlàiiŋ]

13　limitation [lìmitéiʃən]

13　colleague [kάliːg]

13　previously [príːviəsli]

14　a wide variety of ...

19　on top　　　　頂点に

20　evolution [èvəlúːʃən]

25　as compared to ...

26　readily [rédili]

28　generate [dʒénərèit]

28　fatigue [fətíːg]

29　notion [nóuʃən]

31　overall [óuvərɔ̀ːl]（形）

32　reveal [rivíːl]

34　be involved in ...

37　reverse [rivə́ːrs]（名）

入試発展レベル（二次・有名私大）

6　theoretical [θìːərétikəl]

9　mammal [mǽməl]

9　premise [prémis]（名）

13　get around ...

　　　（問題など）を避ける、（問題など）に対処する

20　ecology [ikάlədʒi]

27　contract [kəntrǽkt]（動）

29　immense [iméns]

30　cellular [séljələr]

35　unexplained [ʌ̀niksphéind]

36　comparable [kámpərəbl]

その他

2　muscle cell　　　筋（肉）細胞

2　acceleration [əksèləréiʃən]

　　　　　　　　　　加速

4　fruit fly　　　ミバエ、ショウジョウバエ

6　maximum speed　　最高速度

10　zoologist [zouάlədʒist]　動物学者

10　German Centre for Integrative

　　Biodiversity Research

　　　　　　　　ドイツ総合生物多様性研究センター

14　ectotherm [éktəuθɜ̀ːrm]　外温動物

14　cold-blooded（形）　冷血の、変温の

15　warm-blooded（形）　温血の、恒温の

15　endotherm [éndəuθɜ̀ːrm]　内温動物

16　flyer [fláiər]　　　空を飛ぶもの

18　versus ...　　　…対、…と対比して

19　inverted-U-shaped（形）

　　　　　　　　　　逆 U 字型の

21　biomechanics [bàiəumikǽniks]

　　　　　　　　　生体力学、生物力学

21　joint [dʒɔ́int]　　　関節

23　constraint [kənstréint]　制限、制約

25　muscle fiber　　筋繊維［線維］

33　ecophysiologist [ìːkoufiziάlədʒist]

　　　　　　　　　生態生理学者

35　land animal　　陸生動物、陸の動物

展開	段落	要旨
主題と結論の提示	1	最速の動物はなぜ（①　　　　　）動物ではなく（②　　　　　）動物なのか。この長年の疑問に対する答えが、（①　　　　　）動物の筋細胞が理論上の（③　　　　　　）に達する前に燃料不足になることにある、と新研究が明らかにした。
主題の展開①	2	ヒルト氏は、以前の研究が特定のグループの、限られたサイズの範囲内の動物に焦点を当てていたため、根本的な要因が隠れているかもしれないと指摘する。
主題の展開②	3	ヒルト氏たちは、以前収集された、サイズも生息場所も広範囲にわたる生物のデータを考察した。
主題の展開③	4	（③　　　　　　）と（④　　　　　）をマッピングすると、（②　　　　　）動物が頂点にくる逆Ｕ字型のグラフが得られたが、ヒルト氏によると、これは生物力学とは関連がない。
主題の展開④	5	（②　　　　　）動物が最速になる傾向は根本的な代謝の制約と関連しており、（①　　　　　）動物の「（⑤　　　　　　）」筋繊維は、動物が（③　　　　　　）に到達するのに要する時間よりもずっと短時間でエネルギー源を使い果たしてしまうからだ、と考えられる。
主題の展開⑤	6	今回の研究は、動物の最高速度に影響を与える他の要因を明らかにするきっかけになるかもしれない。

百字要約　　「段落要旨」を参考にして、本文全体の内容を百字程度の日本語で要約しなさい。

（下書き）

本文解説

1 【more of ...】

(l.1) That's because big creatures have **more of** the type of muscle cells used for acceleration.

▶ more of the type of muscle cells used for acceleration で、「より多くの、加速に使われるタイプの筋細胞」。more は、more muscle cells used for acceleration であれば of は不要だが、後に〈the +名詞〉や代名詞などが続くときは more of ... を使う。much of ... や many of ... についても同様である。

ex. I want <u>more of</u> that information in detail.「もっとその詳しい情報がほしい」
He didn't eat <u>much of</u> his breakfast.「彼は朝食をあまり食べなかった」
<u>Many of</u> them were college students.「彼らの多くは大学生だった」

2 【range from A to B】

(l.4) Now, an analysis of nearly 500 species **ranging from** fruit flies **to** whales has an answer: ...

(l.15) The 474 species they considered included runners, swimmers, and flyers that **ranged** in weight **from** 30 micrograms **to** 100 tons.

▶ 上記の 2 つの文中の range はどちらも動詞で、range from A to B で「(範囲などが) A から B に及ぶ」。第 2 文では in weight が加わり、「体重の範囲」であることがはっきり示されている。

ex. The patients ranged in age from 6 to 85.
「患者の年齢は 6 歳から 85 歳までだった」

3 【付帯状況を表す with】

(l.18) When the scientists mapped a creature's top speed versus its weight, they got an inverted-U-shaped graph, **with moderately sized animals on top**, they report today in *Nature Ecology and Evolution*.

▶ with ... on top は、〈with + O(moderately sized animals) + C(on top)〉の形で付帯状況を表している。主節の they got an inverted-U-shaped graph「彼らは逆 U 字型のグラフを得た」に対して、「(そのグラフでは) 中規模の大きさの動物が頂点にきていた」と補足説明を加えている。この構文では O が続く語句の意味上の主語になっていて、ここでは moderately sized animals were on top という関係が成り立つ。

▶ 付帯状況を表す〈with + O + C〉では、C の部分に現在分詞、過去分詞、形容詞、副詞、前置詞句などがくる。

ex. They waited for the cat to come back with the door slightly ajar.
「彼らはドアを少しだけ開けて猫が戻るのを待った」
You must not fuel your car with the engine running.
「エンジンをかけたまま給油してはいけない」

(l.23) Instead, it appears to be related to a much more fundamental metabolic constraint: the length of time required for the animal to reach its theoretical maximum speed, **based on** the number of "fast-twitch" muscle fiber cells in the creature's muscles, **as compared to** the length of time it takes for those cells to run out of readily available energy.

> ▶ コロン (:) 以下は、直前の a much more fundamental metabolic constraint「もっとずっと根本的な代謝の制約」を具体的に説明している。

> ▶ required ... maximum speed は (the length of) time を修飾する過去分詞句。for the animal to reach ... では、the animal が to reach の意味上の主語になっている。「動物がその理論上の最高速度に達するのに必要とされる時間の長さ」

> ▶ based on ... で「…に基づく［基づいて］」。the creature は前の the animal の言い換え。based on ... muscles は its theoretical speed「その理論上の最高速度」について、「動物の筋肉中の『急激に収縮する』筋繊維細胞の数に基づく」と特定している。

> ▶ as compared to ... は「…と比較して」。to の代わりに with が使われることもある。it takes 以下は、直前に関係代名詞 that[which] が省略されていて、(the length of) time を先行詞とする節を導いている。ここでも for A to *do* の形が使われ、those cells が to run の意味上の主語になっている。「それらの細胞がすぐに使えるエネルギーを使い果たしてしまうのにかかる時間の長さと比較したときの」

(l.35) One such unexplained trend is that warm-blooded land animals are usually faster than cold-blooded creatures of comparable size, **whereas** at sea **the reverse is usually true**.

> ▶ whereas は「(その) 一方で、〜であるのに対して」の意味を表す〈比較・対照〉の接続詞。ここでは前半の land animals「陸生動物」と、海に (at sea) すむ動物が比べられている。

> ▶ the reverse は「逆、反対 (のこと)」。at sea the reverse is true で「海ではその逆が真実である」。

Many linguists predict that at least half of the world's 6,000 or so languages will be 🔊11
dead or dying by the year 2050. Languages are becoming extinct at twice the rate of
endangered mammals and four times the rate of endangered birds. If this trend
continues, the world of the future could be dominated by a dozen or fewer languages.

5 Even higher rates of linguistic devastation are possible. Michael Krauss, director of 🔊12
the Alaska Native Language Center, suggests that as many as 90 percent of languages
could become moribund or extinct by 2100. According to Krauss, 20 percent to 40
percent of languages are already moribund, and only 5 percent to 10 percent are "safe"
in the sense of being widely spoken or having official status. If people "become wise
10 and turn it around," Krauss says, the number of dead or dying languages could be
more like 50 percent by 2100 and that's the best-case scenario.

The definition of a healthy language is one that acquires new speakers. No matter 🔊13
how many adults use the language, if it isn't passed to the next generation, its fate is
already sealed. Although a language may continue to exist for a long time as a second
15 or ceremonial language, it is moribund as soon as children stop learning it. For example,
out of twenty native Alaskan languages, only two are still being learned by children.

Although language extinction is sad for the people involved, why should the rest of
us care? What effect will other people's language loss have on the future of people who
speak English, for example? (A)Replacing a minor language with a more widespread
20 one may even seem like a good thing, allowing people to communicate with each other
more easily. But language diversity is as important as biological diversity.

Andrew Woodfield, director of the Centre for Theories of Language and Learning 🔊14
in Bristol, England, suggested in a 1995 seminar on language conservation that people
do not yet know all the ways in which linguistic diversity is important. "The fact is, no
25 one knows exactly what riches are hidden inside the less-studied languages," he says.

Woodfield compares one argument for conserving unstudied endangered plants —
that they may be medically valuable — with the argument for conserving endangered
languages. "We have inductive evidence based on past studies of well-known languages
that there will be riches, even though we do not know what they will be. (B)It seems
30 paradoxical but it's true. By allowing languages to die out, the human race is destroying
things it doesn't understand," he argues.

Stephen Wurm, in his introduction to the Atlas of the World's Languages in Danger 🔊15
of Disappearing, tells (C)the story of one medical cure that depended on knowledge of
a traditional language. Northern Australia experienced an outbreak of severe skin
35 ulcers* that resisted conventional treatment. Aborigines* acquainted with the nurse

told her about a lotion derived from a local medicinal plant that would cure the ulcers. Being a woman of broad experience, the woman didn't dismiss this claim for non-Western medical knowledge. Instead, she applied the lotion, which healed the ulcers.

16 This incident and similar ones have resulted in a general search throughout Australia for medicinal plants known to aboriginal people through their languages and traditional 40 cultures. The search has to be fast because most Australian languages are dying. When they go, the medical knowledge stored in them will go too.

As Michael Krauss expresses it, the web of languages is a "microcosm of highly specialized information. (D)Every language has its own take on the world. One language is not simply a different set of words for the same things." Just as we depend on 45 biological complexity for our physical survival, we depend on linguistic complexity for our cultural survival.

    ★ skin ulcers「皮膚炎」   Aborigines「原住民」

解答欄

1 (1) ....   (2) ....   (3) ....

2
....
....
....

3
....
....
....

4 (1) ....
....
    (2) ....
....

5 ....

6 ....

語句　音声は、「英語」→「日本語の意味」の順で読まれます。　　　　　CD 1- Tr 17-20

入試基礎レベル

6　as many as ...

10　turn ... around

12　definition [dèfəníʃən]

12　acquire [əkwáiər]

18　have effect on ...

19　replace A with B

20　allow A to *do*

26　argument [árɡjumənt]

27　valuable [vǽljəbl]

30　die out

31　argue [árɡju:]（動）

32　introduction [ìntrədʌ́kʃən]

33　depend on ...

34　severe [sivíər]

37　claim [kleim]（名）

39　result in ...

入試標準レベル（共通テスト・私大）

1　predict [pridíkt]

2　extinct [ikstínkt]

3　endangered [indéindʒərd]

4　dominate [dámənèit]

5　linguistic [liŋɡwístik]

9　in the sense of ...

9　status [stéitəs]

13　pass A to B

13　fate [féit]

17　extinction [ikstíŋkʃən]

17　involved [inválvd]

19　widespread [wáidspréd]

21　diversity [dəvə́rsəti]

23　conservation [kànsərvéiʃən]

28　evidence [évidəns]

35　resist [rizíst]

35　conventional [kənvénʃənəl]

35　(be) acquainted with ...

36　(be) derived from ...

37　dismiss A for B

38　heal [hi:l]

39　incident [ínsidənt]

42　(be) stored in ...

入試発展レベル（二次・有名私大）

1　linguist [líŋɡwist]

3　mammal [mǽməl]

5　devastation [dèvəstéiʃən]

14　second language

15　ceremonial [sérəmóuniəl]（形）

26　conserve [kənsə́rv]

33　medical cure

43　web [wéb]

その他

7　moribund [mɔ́ribʌ̀nd]　消滅寸前の、瀕死の

14　seal [sí:l]（動）　決定する

25　riches [rítʃiz]　豊かさ、富、財産

28　inductive [indʌ́ktiv]　帰納的な

30　paradoxical [pæ̀rədáksikəl]　逆説的な

32　atlas [ǽtləs]　地図帳、図鑑

34　outbreak [áutbrèik]　勃発、発生

36　lotion [lóuʃən]　水薬、ローション

36　medicinal plant　薬草、薬用植物

36　ulcer [ʌ́lsər]　潰瘍

43　microcosm [máikrəkà:zəm]　小宇宙

44　have *one*'s own take on ...　…について独自の意見を持つ

46　physical survival　物理的生存

47　cultural survival　文化的生存

展開	段落	要旨
序論①	1	言語の半数が（①　　　　　　　）年までに消滅または消滅寸前となる予想がある。
序論②	2	より速く言語が荒廃する可能性もある。90％が（②　　　　　　　）年までに消滅寸前か消滅するかもしれない。
本論①	3	健全な言語とは、新しい話し手を獲得している言語で、（③　　　　　　　）がその言語を学ばなければすぐに瀕死の状態になる。
本論②	4	言語の消滅は、その言語に関係しない人々には無関係とも思えるが、（④　　　　　　　）は生物の多様性と同様重要である。
本論③	5	（④　　　　　　　　　　）の重要さや未研究言語の豊かさはまだ正確には把握されていない。
本論④	6	よく知られた言語に関する過去の研究から、消滅寸前の言語にも豊かなものがあるはずだ、と推論できる。
本論⑤	7	オーストラリアで、従来の（⑤　　　　　　）が効かない皮膚潰瘍が、地元の人々が知っていた薬草から取れるローションで治癒した。
本論⑥	8	言語の消滅は、言語に蓄積されている（⑥　　　　　　　）知識の消滅も意味する。
結論	9	言語が織りなす言語網は情報の小宇宙で、人間は文化的な生存を（④　　　　　　　）に依存している。

百字要約　　「段落要旨」を参考にして、本文全体の内容を百字程度の日本語で要約しなさい。

（下書き）

（方眼用紙　10　20）

（方眼用紙　10　20）

2.

本文解説

1　【out of ...】

(l.15)　For example, **out of twenty** native Alaskan languages, **only two** are still being learned by children.

▶ out of ... は「（ある数）のうちで、（ある数）の中から」の意味を表す。Only two out of twenty native Alaskan languages are still being learned by children. と表現することもできる。「アラスカ先住民の20ある言語のうちで、今でも子どもたちが学んでいる言語はたったの2言語にすぎない」という意味。
　　ex. It has been said that nine out of ten people like chocolate and the tenth one is lying.
　　「10人中9人はチョコレートが好きで、10人目は嘘をついている、と言われている」

2　【The fact is, ...】

(l.24)　"**The fact is**, no one knows exactly what riches are hidden inside the less-studied languages," he says.

▶ Fact is that ... や The fact is that ... は「実を言うと…である、実情は…である」の意味。この例のように that を用いずに The fact is, ... のような形もある。The truth is, ... も同様の意味を表す。
　　ex. The cruel truth is, he will never recover.「むごいことだが、彼の回復の見込みはない」

3　【文構造】【compare A with B】

(l.26)　Woodfield **compares** one argument for conserving unstudied endangered plants — **that** they may be medically valuable — **with** the argument for conserving endangered languages.

▶ with が離れているが、compare A with B「AとBを比較する、対照する」の形。
▶ ダッシュにはさまれた that 節は one argument の具体的内容である。「未研究の絶滅危惧植物には医学的な価値があるかもしれないという（主張)」

4　【文構造】【同格節を導く that】

(l.28)　We have inductive evidence based on past studies of well-known languages **that** there will be riches, even though we do not know what they will be.

▶ that 以下は inductive evidence の同格節で、「帰納的証拠」の具体的内容を述べている。「私たちは…という帰納的証拠を持っている」という意味。
▶ based on past studies of well-known languages「よく知られた言語に関する過去の研究に基づいた」は直前の inductive evidence を修飾している。
▶ inductive < induction「帰納（法）」　induction は英英辞典で次のように説明されている。
　Induction is a method of reasoning in which you use individual ideas or facts to give you a general rule or conclusion.
　「帰納とは、個々の考えや事実から一般的な規則や結論を得る推理法のことである」
▶ riches「豊かさ、富、財産」

5　【instead】

(l.37)　Being a woman of broad experience, the woman didn't dismiss this claim for non-Western medical knowledge. **Instead**, she applied the lotion, which healed the ulcers.

▶ Instead は前文を受けて「その代わりに、そうはせずに、それよりむしろ、それどころか」。ここでは Instead of dismissing this claim for non-Western medical knowledge「看護師はこの（＝ローションについての先住民の）主張を非西洋医学的な知識だとして退けるようなことはせずに」の意味。

Memo

A sari for a month. It shouldn't have been a big deal but it was. After all, I had grown up around women wearing saris in India. My mother even slept in one.

In India, saris are adult clothes. After I turned eighteen, I occasionally wore a beautiful sari for weddings and holidays and to the temple. But wearing a silk sari to 5 an Indian party was one thing. Deciding to wear a sari every day while living in New York, especially after ten years in Western clothes, seemed (1)outrageous, even to me.

The sari is six yards of fabric folded into a graceful yet impractical garment. It is fragile and can fall apart at any moment. When worn right, it is supremely elegant and feminine.

10 It requires (2a), however. No longer could I spring across the street just before the light changed. The sari forced me to shorten my strides. I had to throw my shoulders back and pay attention to my posture. I couldn't squeeze into a crowded subway car for fear that someone would accidentally pull my sari. I couldn't balance four bags from the supermarket in one hand and pull out my house keys from a 15 convenient pocket with the other. By the end of the first week, I was feeling frustrated and angry with myself. What was I trying to (3a)?

The notion of wearing a sari every day was relatively new for me. During my college years — the age when most girls in India begin wearing saris regularly — I was studying in America as an art student and I wore casual clothes just as other students 20 did. After getting married, I became a housewife experimenting with more fashionable clothes. Over the years, in short, I tried to talk, walk, and act like an (4).

Then I moved to New York and became a mother. I wanted to teach my three-year-old daughter Indian values and traditions because I knew she would be profoundly different from the children she would play with in religion (we are Hindus), eating 25 habits (we are vegetarians), and the festivals we celebrated. (A)Wearing a sari every day was my way of showing her that she could melt into the pot while keeping her individual flavor.

It wasn't just for my daughter's sake that I decided to wear a sari. I was tired of trying to (3b). No American singers had ever spoken to me as deeply as my favorite 30 Indian singers. Nor could I sing popular American songs as easily as I could my favorite Indian tunes. Much as I enjoyed American food, I couldn't last four days without an Indian meal. It was time to show my ethnicity with a sari and a bright red bindi*. I was going to be an (5a), but on my own terms. It was America's turn to adjust to me.

35 Slowly, I eased into wearing the garment. I owned it and it owned me. Strangers stared at me as I walked proudly across a crowded bookstore. Some of them caught my eye and smiled. At first, I resented being an (5b). Then I wondered: perhaps I reminded them of a wonderful holiday in India or a favorite Indian cookbook. Shop

assistants pronounced their words clearly when they spoke to me. Everywhere, I was stopped with questions about India as if wearing a sari had made me an (5c). One Japanese lady near Times Square asked to have her picture taken with me. (B)<u>A tourist had thought that I was one, too, just steps from my home.</u>

27　　But there were unexpected (2b). Indian taxi drivers raced across lanes and stopped in front of me just as I stepped into the street to hail a cab. When my daughter climbed high up the jungle gym in Central Park, I gathered my sari and prepared to follow, hoping it wouldn't balloon out like Marilyn Monroe's dress. One of the dads standing nearby saw that I was in trouble and volunteered to climb after her. (6)<u>A knight in New York?</u> Was it me? Or was it my sari?

28　　Best of all, my family approved. My husband praised me. My parents were proud of me. My daughter gave out a sigh of admiration when I pulled out my colorful saris. When I hugged her tenderly in my arms, scents from the small bag of sweet-smelling herbs that I used to freshen my sari at night escaped from the folds of cloth and calmed her to sleep. (C)<u>I felt part of a long line of Indian mothers who had rocked their babies this way.</u>

29　　Soon, the month was over. My self-imposed (2c) was coming to an end. Instead of feeling liberated, I felt a sharp pain of unease. I had started to (3c) my sari.

　　Saris were impractical for America, I told myself. I would continue to wear them but not every day. It was time to go back to my sensible casual clothes.

　　＊　bindi「ヒンドゥー教徒の女性が額につける印」

解答欄

1　　..........................

2　(2a) ....　　(2b) ....　　(2c) ....

3　(3a) ....　　(3b) ....　　(3c) ....

4　　..

5　　..........................

6　　..........................

7　　..

8　　..

次ページへ続く→

3.

9 ....

10 ....

| 語句 | 音声は、「英語」→「日本語の意味」の順で読まれます。 | CD 1- Tr 30-33 |

入試基礎レベル

3 turn ... .

11 force ... to *do* ....

12 pay attention to ... .

16 prove [pru:v] ....

18 regularly [régjulərli] ....

20 experiment with ... .

27 individual [ìndəvídʒuəl] (形) ....

....

27 flavor [fléivər] ....

28 be tired of ... .

29 fit in ....

34 adjust to ... .

35 own [óun] (動) ....

36 stare at ... .

38 remind ... of ~ ....

43 advantage [ədvǽntidʒ] ....

45 gather [gǽðər] ....

49 best of all ....

49 approve [əprú:v] ....

49 praise [préiz] (動) ....

52 escape from ... .

52 calm [kɑ:m] (動) ....

55 come to an end ....

入試標準レベル（共通テスト・私大）

3 occasionally [əkéiʒənəli] ....

7 fold [fóuld] ....

8 fall apart ....

10 sacrifice [sǽkrəfàis] (名) ....

13 accidentally [ǽksidénttəli] ....

15 frustrated [frʌstréitəd] ....

17 notion [nóuʃən] ....

21 in short ....

23 profoundly [prəfáundli] ....

25 celebrate [séləbrèit] ....

26 melt into ... .

28 for *one*'s sake ....

31 tune [tú:n] ....

31 last [lǽst] (動) ....

33 immigrant [ímigrənt] ....

37 exhibit [igzíbit] (名) ....

39 pronounce [prənáuns] ....

43 unexpected [ʌnikspéktəd] ....

44 step into ... .

47 volunteer to *do* ....

50 sigh [sái] ....

50 admiration [ædməréiʃən] ....

51 hug [hʌg] (動) ....

55 be over ....

55 self-imposed ....

55 obligation [àbligéiʃən] ....

56 liberated [líbərèitid] ....

58 sensible [sénsəbəl] ....

7	**fabric** [fǽbrik]		1	**big deal**	重大事、大ごと
7	**graceful** [gréisfl]		6	**outrageous** [autréidʒəs]	
7	**impractical** [imprǽktikəl]				途方もない、常軌を逸した
			7	**yard** [járd]	ヤード（長さの単位）
8	**fragile** [frǽdʒəl]		7	**garment** [gármənt]	衣服、衣類
9	**feminine** [fémənin]		8	**supremely** [suprí:mli]	最高に、この上なく
10	**spring across ...**		11	**stride** [stráid]	歩幅
	飛び跳ねるようにして…を渡る		11	**throw** *one's* **shoulders back**	
11	**shorten** [ʃɔ́rtən]				そり身になる、胸を張る
12	**squeeze into ...**		12	**posture** [pástʃər]	姿勢
32	**ethnicity** [eθnísiti]		35	**ease into ...**	…に徐々に慣れる
33	**on** *one's* **own terms**	自分の思い通りの条件で	44	**hail a cab**	タクシーを呼び止める
37	**resent** [rizént]		51	**tenderly** [téndərli]	優しく、そっと
40	**authority** [əθɔ́:rəti]		52	**herb** [ə́:rb]	ハーブ
43	**race across ...**	急いで…を横切る	53	**rock** [rák]（動）	優しく揺する、揺り動かす
46	**balloon out**	（風船のように）膨らむ	56	**unease** [ʌníz]（名）	不安、精神的不快
51	**scent** [sént]				
53	**line** [láin]	系統、家系			

3.

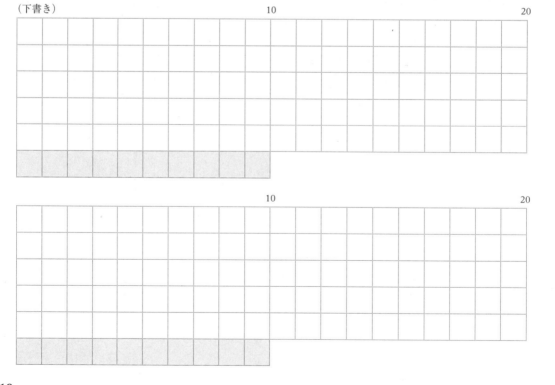

展開	段落	要旨
導入①	1	（①　　　　　　）の間サリーを着るのは、実際には大ごとだった。
導入②	2	長く洋服で生活したあと、ニューヨークで毎日サリーを着ることは、途方もないことに思えた。
導入③	3	サリーは優美だが、実用的ではない衣服だ。
展開①	4	サリーを着て過ごすことにはさまざまな（②　　　　　）が伴った。
展開②	5	（③　　　　　　　）のように振る舞おうとしてきた私にとって、サリーを着るという考えは新しいものだった。
展開③	6	サリーを着ることで、（④　　　）に個性を保ったままで（⑤　　　　　　　　）に溶け込めることを示したかったのだ。
展開④	7	私がサリーを着ようと決めたのは、（④　　　）のためだけではなかった。周りに適応しようとすることにうんざりしていたのだ。
展開⑤	8	サリーを着ることには徐々に慣れていった。初めは見世物になっていることに憤慨したが、次第に好意的な目で見られているのかもしれないと考えるようになった。
展開⑥	9	思いがけない利得もあり、インド人のタクシー運転手から、また公園である男性から親切にしてもらうこともあった。
展開⑦	10	何よりもよかったのは、（⑥　　　　　　）が私のサリーを褒め、誇りに思ってくれたことだった。
展開⑧	11	1か月が終わったが、私はサリーを楽しみ始めていた。
展開⑨	12	実用的な服に戻るべきときだった。

18

Memo

本文解説

▣ 【one thing ... (another)】

(l.4) But wearing a silk sari to an Indian party was **one thing**. Deciding to wear a sari every day while living in New York, especially after ten years in Western clothes, seemed outrageous, even to me.

- ▸ サリーに囲まれて育ち、サリーを着て結婚式や寺院などに行くことがあった筆者が、「絹のサリーをインド式のパーティーに着ていく」ことと、「ニューヨークで暮らしながら毎日サリーを着ようと決意する」ことを対比している。

- ▸ 第1文は後続の文に another という語はないが、A is one thing, but B is (quite) another.「AとBは（全く）別だ」という構文が下敷きになっている。"A is one thing, but B is another." is used to indicate that the second item mentioned is much more important than the first, and cannot be compared to it. という英英辞典の説明からもわかるように、another に当たる部分には one thing に比べて困難や重要性、あるいは極端の程度がより大きな内容がくる。ここでは、another に当たる outrageous「途方もない、とんでもない」に対し、one thing は「たいしたことではない」といった意味で使われている。

▣ 【倒置】

(l.10) **No longer could I spring** across the street just before the light changed.

(l.30) **Nor could I sing** popular American songs as easily as I could my favorite Indian tunes.

- ▸ 第1文は、no longer「もはや…でない」という否定表現が強調のために文頭に置かれたために、続く部分で主語と助動詞が倒置されて「疑問文と同じ形」could I spring になっている。「私はもう、信号が変わる直前に通りを跳ねながら渡ることはできなかった」 spring across ...「飛び跳ねるようにして…を渡る」

- ▸ 第2文も、nor「…もまたない」という否定語が文頭に置かれたために、続く部分が could I sing と倒置の形になっている。「また私も、アメリカで人気の歌を、私の大好きなインドの曲ほど気楽に歌うこともできなかった」

▣ 【文構造】【melt into the pot】

(l.25) Wearing a sari every day was my way of showing her that she could **melt into the pot** while keeping her individual flavor.

- ▸ Wearing a sari every day が主部、my way 以下が was の補語。my way of showing that ...「…ということを示す私なりのやり方」 while keeping ...「…を保ったままで」

- ▸ melt into the pot「つぼの中に溶け込む（→多種多様な人種、民族、文化などが存在する社会に混じり合って同化することを表す比喩的表現）」 melting pot は a place where people from different races, countries, or social classes come to live together のことを指し、特にアメリカやニューヨークはよく melting pot「（人種や文化などの）るつぼ」に例えられる。最近では、混ぜても溶け合わないまま並立共存している状況を指して、salad bowl「サラダボウル」という表現も使われている。

- ▸ flavor には「特色、持ち味」の意味もあり、her individual flavor で「彼女（＝筆者の娘）が持つ個性」。

4 　【own の用法】
_____

(l.35)　Slowly, I eased into wearing the garment. I **owned** it and it **owned** me.

▸ own は動詞で「所有する、自分のものにする」の意味。この文は「私はサリーを所有し、サリーは私を所有した」が直訳だが、直前の「ゆっくりと、私はこの衣装を着ることに慣れていった」から判断すると、「私はサリーになじんでいったし」、また「サリーの方でも私を受け入れてくれた」と、サリーが筆者にしっくりくるようになってきたことを擬人的に表現していることが読み取れる。別な表現をすれば The sari and I became a part of each other. とも言えるだろう。

5　【話法】【knight】【it の用法】
_____

(l.46)　One of the dads standing nearby saw that I was in trouble and volunteered to climb after her. **A knight in New York? Was it me? Or was it my sari?**

▸ 第2～4文は、筆者が心の中で思ったことをそのまま表現する描出話法と呼ばれる話法で書かれている。描出話法とは「直接話法と間接話法の中間的な話法で、例えば He said などを省略して、被伝達部分を独立させて地の文に埋め込み、登場人物の発言や考えなどを表現する用法」。小説などによく見られる。第3～4文を間接話法で書けば、I wondered if it was me or it was my sari. などとなるだろう。この文章には何か所か描出話法が見られる。第4段落最終文の What was I trying to prove? もその1つで、これも直接話法で書けば" What am I trying to prove?" I said to myself. などとなる。

▸ 第2文の「ニューヨークに現れた knight かしら？」とは、サリーを着たまま娘を追いかけようとしていた筆者の代わりにジャングルジムに登る役を買って出てくれた1人の父親をユーモラスに knight と表現したもの。knight は「中世の騎士」だが、英語で a knight in shining armor「輝く甲冑（かっちゅう）を着た騎士」と言えば a man who is kind and brave, and is likely to rescue you from a difficult situation のことで、特に「女性の保護者」という意味が強い。

▸ 第3、4文の it は「状況の it」と言われる用法で、ここでは第1文に述べられている内容を指している。Was it because of me that the dad volunteered to climb after my daughter? Or was it because of my sari?「その父親が娘を追いかける役を買ってくれたのは、私のせいかしら？ それとも私のサリーのせいかしら？」といった意味。

How do migrating birds find their way? First we must ask, what possible clues are there? If birds are flying over land, where there are features below that are distinct and stay the same for year after year — rivers, roads, forests, coastlines — then, of course, they can use their eyes. There is plenty of evidence that (1)birds do just this. Many, for
5 example, follow coastlines and thread their way through straits and mountain passes.

When they get very close to where they want to be, many use their sense of smell. 35 Homing pigeons give a clue to this. ("Homing" is not the same as migration. It suggests that pigeons can find their way home when taken by train or truck to some far-distant place and then released. But homing surely has some of the same mechanisms as
10 migration does, and so can give clues to how it works.) It seems that as pigeons get fairly close to their home, they first pick up general smells that tell of bird dwellings — perhaps the general tempting stink of ammonia. As they get nearer, the smells become more specifically pigeon-like. Finally, as they get very close, they recognize the very particular odor of their own flock in its own space. More and more evidence is revealing that
15 humans, too, have a wonderful awareness of odor, even if they do not consciously recognize it, such that they find particular men or women attractive or disgusting according to their primitive substances such as sweat: no doubt a cooling thought for those who like to suppose that (2)human beings have risen above such things. We do not normally think of birds as creatures that attach importance to smell, but many of them
20 do, in many contexts.

But what use are (A) clues when a bird is above some apparently boundless ocean? 36 What value is (B) when it is a thousand miles from where it wants to be? What else is there?

Quite a lot, is the answer. On the visual front, there is the sun by day and the moon 37
25 and stars by night. These are hard to make good use of unless the bird also has some sense of time, so it knows where the sun or the moon ought to be at a particular time; but birds do have a sense of time.

Human beings navigate by the heavenly bodies, too, but we make a great science of it. 38 The skills of the navigator were among the most complex and prized in all the world's
30 navies until well into the nineteenth century, when sailors in danger could find out where they were by radio. Traditional long-distance sailors needed telescopes and charts, and pages and pages of tables, to help them work out where they were. Birds have to do all this in their heads, in their bird brains, on the wing. The problem conceptually is the same as we meet in discussing the diving of fish-eating seabirds (how they always fold
35 their wings at exactly the right time). In each case the math is immensely complicated, once you spell it out. But presumably birds on the wing, not familiar with mathematics, don't spell it out. (3)They must have some practical rules that instantly translate the cues

that are offered by the sun and stars and moon into directives for purposeful action.

&39   Again, there are clues and stories that seem to be throwing some light. For instance, (4)many kinds of birds are known to use star maps. In the early weeks of life the baby 40 birds sit in their nests and study the night sky — and are somewhat confused if those early weeks are too cloudy. But they do not, as human amateur astronomers might do, spend their time learning the individual constellations★ — how to recognize Orion★ or trace the fanciful outline of Taurus★, or whatever. Instead, they focus on the part that does not move as the night progresses, which in the Northern Hemisphere means the 45 North Star. They can see, if they look at it long enough, that as the night progresses, all the stars in the sky, including the mighty Orion and the notional Taurus, seem to revolve around the Pole Star, which sits in the middle like the central part of a giant cartwheel. Once they recognize the central part, the most fundamental problem is solved. The creature that can do this knows where north is and everything else can be figured out. I 50 don't know what the equivalent would be in the Southern Hemisphere, but undoubtedly there is one. Navigation simply does not seem to need the details of astronomy.

   ★ constellation「星座」 Orion「オリオン座」 Taurus「牡牛座」

解答欄

1
....
....

2 (A) ....   (B) ....

3
....
....
....

4
....
....
....

5
....
....
....
....

6
....

4.

語句　音声は、「英語」→「日本語の意味」の順で読まれます。　CD 1- Tr 40-43

入試基礎レベル

16 **attractive** [ətrǽktiv] ....

21 **apparently** [əpǽrəntli] ....

42 **amateur** [ǽmətʃùər] ....

43 **individual** [ìndəvídʒuəl]（形）......................

....

45 **progress** [prəgrés]（動）......................

49 **fundamental** [fʌ̀ndəméntəl] ....

....

入試標準レベル（共通テスト・私大）

1 **clue** [klú:] ....

2 **distinct** [distíŋkt] ....

4 **evidence** [évidəns] ....

13 **specifically** [spəsífikəli] ....

14 **flock** [flák] ....

14 **reveal** [riví:l]（動）......................

15 **awareness** [əwéərnəs] ....

15 **consciously** [kánʃəsli] ....

16 **disgusting** [disgʌ́stiŋ] ....

17 **primitive** [prímətiv] ....

19 **creature** [krí:tʃər] ....

19 **attach importance to ...**

....

20 **context** [kántekst] ....

25 **make good use of ...**

31 **chart** [tʃárt]　　海図

35 **complicated** [kámpləkèitid]

....

36 **spell out ...**

37 **translate ... into ～**

41 **nest** [nést] ....

44 **trace** [tréis]（動）......................

44 **focus on ...**

47 **notional** [nóuʃənəl] ....

50 **figure out ...**

51 **equivalent** [ikwívələnt] ....

52 **simply ... not**

入試発展レベル（二次・有名私大）

7 **migration** [maigréiʃən] ....

10 **fairly** [féərli] ....

11 **dwelling** [dwéliŋ]（名）......................

12 **tempting** [témptiŋ] ....

14 **odor** [óudər] ....

21 **boundless** [báundləs] ....

28 **heavenly body** ....

33 **conceptually** [kənséptʃuəli] ....

....

35 **immensely** [iménsli] ....

37 **cue** [kjú:]（名）......................

38 **purposeful** [pə́:rpəsfl] ....

42 **astronomer** [əstránəmər] ....

45 **the Northern Hemisphere**

....

45 **the North Star**

47 **mighty** [máiti]（形）......................

51 **the Southern Hemisphere**

....

51 **undoubtedly** [ʌndáutidli] ....

52 **astronomy** [əstránəmi] ....

その他

1 **migrating bird**　　渡り鳥

5 **thread** *one*'s **way**　　縫うように進む

5 **strait** [stréit]　　海峡

7 **homing pigeon**　　伝書バト

12 **stink** [stíŋk]（名）　　悪臭

12 **ammonia** [əmóunjə]　　アンモニア

28 **navigate** [nǽvigèit]（動）　航海する

29 **prized** [práizd]（形）

極めて重要な、珍重される

34 **fold** *one*'s **wings**　　（鳥が）翼を畳む

36 **presumably** [prizú:məbli] おそらく

38 **directive** [dəréktiv]（名）　指示、命令

39 **throw light**

解明を助ける、手がかりを与える

44 **fanciful** [fǽnsifl]　　空想的な、奇抜な

48 **cartwheel** [ká:rthwì:l]　　車輪

52 **details** [dí:teilz]　　〔複数形で〕詳細（な情報）

展開	段落	要旨
序論①	1	渡り鳥の進路の見つけ方を知るには、（①　　　　　　）を探す必要がある。鳥が陸地の上を飛ぶときには、（②　　　　）を使って進路を見つけている。
序論②	2	多くの鳥は、目的地の近くでは（③　　　　　）を使う。伝書バトは、巣に近づくと鳥のすみかの匂いをとらえ、すぐ近くまで来ると、自分たちの群れ特有の匂いを嗅ぎ分ける。
本論①	3	鳥が海の上を飛ぶとき、目的地から遠いとき、視覚や匂いに価値があるだろうか。
本論②	4	視覚的な面では（④　　　　　）や月、星があり、それを利用するための（⑤　　　　　）の感覚を鳥は持っている。
本論③	5	人間は望遠鏡や海図などを用い、（⑥　　　　　）を頼りに航海していたが、鳥は（⑥　　　　　）からの情報を目的に合う行動に直ちに変換する法則を持っているに違いない。
結論	6	その解明への手がかりは、多くの鳥が（⑦　　　　　）を使うということである。生後数週間の鳥のヒナは、夜空を観察し、北半球の（⑧　　　　　）を認識する。それができれば北の方向がわかり、その他すべてのことも理解できるのである。

百字要約　　「段落要旨」を参考にして、本文全体の内容を百字程度の日本語で要約しなさい。

（下書き）

10　　　　　　　　　　　　　　　　20

（空欄の原稿用紙）

10　　　　　　　　　　　　　　　　20

（空欄の原稿用紙）

4.

本文解説

1 　【文構造】【such that 〜】【no doubt】

(l.14) More and more evidence is revealing that humans, too, have a wonderful awareness of odor, even if they do not consciously recognize it, **such that** they find particular men or women attractive or disgusting according to their primitive substances such as sweat: **no doubt** a cooling thought for those who like to suppose that human beings have risen above such things.

▶ 「ますます多くの証拠が明らかにしている」のは、that humans 以下 such as sweat までの内容。

▶ この文の such that 〜は、前出の照応する語句と同格的に「〜のようなもの、〜するほどのもの」の意味を表す。ここでは a wonderful awareness of odor を受け、人間の嗅覚のすばらしさについて「例えば、特定の人を魅力的だ、気持ち悪いなどと感じたりするような匂いの認識力」または「特定の人を魅力的だ、気持ち悪いなどと感じたりするほどの匂いの認識力」。

▶ no doubt a cooling thought for ... は、no doubt (it will [must] be) a cooling thought for ... と省略されている語句を補って読む。it が指すのは、that humans 以下コロン(:)の前までの内容である。cooling は throwing cold water on ... の意味で、日本語の「冷や水を浴びせるような」に当たる。なお、出題英文の原文では a sobering thought「酔いもさめるような考え」となっている。

2 　【make good use of ...】【so の用法】

(l.25) These are hard to **make good use of** unless the bird also has some sense of time, **so** it knows where the sun or the moon ought to be at a particular time; but birds do have a sense of time.

▶ These = the sun and the moon and stars。make good use of ...「…を有効に使う、十分活用する」These are hard to make good use of は、It is hard to make good use of these「そういったものを十分活用するのは難しい」の these を主語にした文。make good use of ... は前置詞を伴う動詞句なので、最後に of が残っていることに注意。

▶ so は「その結果、そのため (= so that)」。so it knows ... particular time も unless に続く内容で、unless 以下は「鳥も時間の感覚を持っていて、特定の時間に太陽あるいは月がどこにあるはずかを知っている、ということでなければ」。

3 　【among the 最上級】【well into ...】【関係副詞の非制限用法】

(l.29) The skills of the navigator were **among the most complex and prized** in all the world's navies until **well into** the nineteenth century, **when** sailors in danger could find out where they were by radio.

▶ 〈among the 最上級（＋名詞)〉＝〈one of the 最上級（＋名詞)〉　among the most complex and prized skills「最も複雑で、高く評価される技術の1つ」。

▶ この into は「(ある期間) に入り込んで」、well は「かなり、だいぶ」の意味。until well into the nineteenth century「19世紀もだいぶ進むまで (≒ until the mid- to late-19th century)」

▶ when ... は関係副詞の非制限 [継続] 用法で、直前の well into the nineteenth century を受け、「そしてその頃には船乗りたちは〜できた」の意味。

(*l.46*) They can see, if they look at it long enough, that as the night progresses, (S')all the stars in the sky, including the mighty Orion and the notional Taurus, (V')seem to revolve around the Pole Star, which sits in the middle like the central part of a giant cartwheel.

> ▶ この文は、If they look at it long enough, they can see that 〜. 「鳥たちは、十分長く眺めていれば〜がわかる」と書き換えられる。

> ▶ that 節中の主部は all the stars in the sky、述語動詞は seem。続く which の先行詞は the Pole Star。

> ▶ as the night progresses「夜が更けるにつれて」　including ...「…を含む」
> notional = conceptual or imaginative

The distribution of educational opportunity plays a key role in shaping human development prospects. Within countries, governments and people increasingly recognize that unequal opportunities for education are linked to inequalities in income, health and wider life chances. And (1)<u>what is true within countries is true also</u>
5 <u>between countries</u>. Large global gaps in education reinforce the extreme divides between rich and poor nations in income, health and other aspects of human development.

The full extent of the gulf in opportunities for education is not widely appreciated. 🎧 45
Education is a universal human right. However, enjoyment of that right is heavily
10 conditioned by birth and inherited circumstance. Access to education is greatly influenced by where one is born and by other factors over which children have no control, including parental income and nationality.

From a global perspective, being born in a developing country is a strong indicator 🎧 46
for reduced opportunity. (2)<u>School achievement, measured in terms of the average</u>
15 <u>number of years or grade reached in education, is one (admittedly limited) measure</u>
<u>of global inequality.</u> While almost all member countries of the Organisation for Economic Co-operation and Development (OECD) have attained universal school achievement to grade 9, most countries in developing regions are far from this position. At age 16, over 80% of the population of the OECD countries is in
20 secondary school while one-quarter of sub-Saharan* Africa's population is still in primary school. Four years later, at age 20, around 30% of the OECD population is in post-secondary education. The figure for sub-Saharan Africa is 2%.

(3)<u>Striking as they are, these figures tell only part of the story.</u> One way of thinking 🎧 47
<u>about unequal opportunity is to consider the chance that a child born in one country</u>
25 <u>will achieve a given level of education relative to a child born somewhere else.</u> The results are revealing. They show that children in countries such as Mali and Mozambique have less chance of completing primary school than children in France or the United Kingdom have of reaching higher education. The gulf in attainment is not restricted to sub-Saharan Africa. Around one in five pupils entering primary
30 school in Latin America and in South and West Asia does not survive to the last primary grade.

Global inequalities in education mirror inequalities in income. The association is 🎧 48
not coincidental. While the relationship between education and wealth creation is complex, knowledge has an important influence on economic growth and productivity.
35 In an increasingly knowledge-based international economy, differences in educational

opportunities are taking on more importance. $_{(4)}$There is a growing sense in which today's inequalities in education can be seen as a predictor for tomorrow's inequalities in the global distribution of wealth, and in opportunities for health and employment. $_{(5)}$The fact that in half the countries of sub-Saharan Africa the survival rate to the last grade of primary school is 67% or less is not irrelevant to prospects for overcoming the region's marginalization in the global economy.

40

★ sub-Saharan「サハラ以南の」

1

....
....
....

2

....
....
....

3

....
....
....
....

4

....
....
....

5

....
....
....
....

5.

入試基礎レベル

1 **opportunity** [àpərtʃúnəti]

1 **shape** [ʃéip] （動）

3 **be linked to ...**

3 **income** [ínkʌm]

8 **extent** [ekstént]

8 **appreciate** [əprí:ʃièit]

14 **measure** [méʒər] （動）

22 **figure** [fígjər]

25 **relative to ...**

27 **complete** [kəmplít]

32 **mirror** [mírər] （動）

34 **have an influence on ...**

入試標準レベル （共通テスト・私大）

1 **distribution** [dìstribjú:ʃən]

2 **prospect** [prá:spèkt] （名）

3 **unequal** [ʌní:kwəl]

5 **gap** [gǽp]

5 **reinforce** [rì:infórs]

5 **extreme** [ikstrí:m]

6 **aspect** [ǽspekt]

9 **universal** [jùnəvə́rsəl]

10 **inherit** [inhérət]

10 **circumstance** [sə́rkəmstæns]

10 **access to ...**

12 **nationality** [næ̀ʃənǽləti]

13 **perspective** [pərspéktiv] （名）

14 **achievement** [ətʃí:vmənt]

14 **in terms of ...**

15 **admittedly** [ədmítidli]

17 **attain** [ətéin]

21 **primary school**

23 **striking** [stráikiŋ]

26 **revealing** [riví:liŋ]

28 **attainment** [ətéinmənt]

29 **(be) restricted to ...**

29 **pupil** [pjú:pl]

32 **association** [əsòusiéiʃən]

34 **complex** [kɑmpléks] （形）

34 **productivity** [pròudʌktívəti]

36 **take on importance**

40 **irrelevant to ...**

入試発展レベル （二次・有名私大）

3 **inequality** [ìnikwɔ́ləti]

5 **divide** [diváid] （名）

10 **condition** [kəndíʃən] （動）

12 **parental** [pəréntəl]

13 **indicator** [índikèitər]

25 **given** [gívn] （形）

33 **coincidental** [kouìnsədéntəl]

その他

8 **gulf** [gʌ́lf]　　格差、大きな隔たり

9 **enjoyment** [indʒɔ́imənt]

享受、恩恵にあずかること

16 **the Organisation for Economic Co-operation and Development**

経済協力開発機構

22 **post-secondary education**

中等後教育

35 **knowledge-based** （形）

知識ベースの、知識集約型の

37 **predictor for ...**

…を占うもの、…の予測の判断材料

39 **survival rate**　　残存率、生存率

41 **marginalization** [mà:rdʒnələzéiʃən]

周辺化、疎外化

展開	段落	要旨
主題の提示 （結論）	1	（①　　　　　　）で（②　　　　　　　）格差が機会の不平等を生むように、国家間の （②　　　　　　）格差もさまざまな面での国家間格差を作り出している。
本論①	2	（②　　　　　　）は（③　　　　　　　　）人権であるが、その権利の享受は出生、継承した 環境などの諸要因によって大きく左右される。
本論②	3	（④　　　　　　　　　）に生まれることは（②　　　　　　）機会の減少を意味し、数字 的にも（②　　　　　　）機会が著しく少ないことが裏付けられている。
本論③	4	機会の不平等は到達（②　　　　　　）水準の格差からも考えることができ、（④ 　　　　　　）と OECD 諸国との差は驚くほど大きい。
結論	5	（②　　　　　　）格差は（⑤　　　　　　）の格差を反映し、知識集約型の（⑥　　　　　　　　　） ではますます重要性を帯びている。

（下書き）　　　　　　　　　　　　　　　　　　　　　　10　　　　　　　　　　　　　　　　　　20

　　　　　　　　　　　　　　　　　　　　　　10　　　　　　　　　　　　　　　　　　20

本文解説

1 【over の用法】

(l.10) Access to education is greatly influenced by where one is born and by other factors **over which** children have no control, including parental income and nationality.

▶ which の先行詞は other factors なので、over については children have no control over other factors から考える。have control over ...「…を制御する、管理する」。other factors over which children have no control「子どもにはどうすることもできないその他の要因」

▶ この over は「〜を支配して、〜の上位に」の意味。

ex. Genghis Khan ruled over an empire stretching from Persia across to China.
「ジンギス・カンはペルシャから中国に至る帝国を支配した」

2 【形容詞（副詞）＋ as ＋ S ＋ V ...】

(l.23) **Striking as they are**, these figures tell only part of the story.

▶ Striking as they are = Though they(= these figures) are striking 〈形容詞（副詞）＋ as ＋ S ＋ V ...〉は「…だけれども」と譲歩の意味を表す。

▶ アメリカ英語では As striking as they are ... のように、形容詞（副詞）の前にさらに as をつける用法もある。

ex. As cold as it was, we went hiking.
「寒かったが、僕らはハイキングに出かけた」

3 【文構造】

(l.23) (S)One way of thinking about unequal opportunity (V)is (C)to consider the chance that a child born in one country will achieve a given level of education / relative to a child born somewhere else.

▶ 全体の構造は上記のとおり。全体は「S は〜の可能性を考えてみることだ」。

▶ the chance that ...「…という可能性」 この that は同格を表す。

▶ relative to a child born somewhere else は「他の場所に生まれた子どもと比べて」。

4 【比較構文】【省略】

(l.26) They show that children in countries such as Mali and Mozambique have **less** chance of completing primary school **than** children in France or the United Kingdom have of reaching higher education.

▶ that 節中は less ... than 〜 の比較構文。children in A have a chance of completing primary school と children in B have of reaching higher education との比較なので、children in B have (a chance) of reaching higher education のように chance を補って読む。less とあるので、前者の可能性の方が少ないのである。

(l.39) **(S)**The fact that / in half the countries of sub-Saharan Africa / the survival rate to the last grade of primary school is 67% or less **(V)**is **(C)**not irrelevant to prospects for overcoming the region's marginalization in the global economy.

▸ 全体の構造は上記のとおりで、that 節中の構造は、(s)the survival rate to the last grade of primary school (v)is (c)67% or less である。

Abraham Darby arrived in Coalbrookdale* with a mission in mind: to produce cheap iron using coal — in the form of coke — as a fuel. His success was foundational to the Industrial Revolution, allowing the production of less expensive iron and so enabling the construction of railways, steamships and industrial machinery, not to

5 mention the famous iron bridge built by Darby's grandson near Coalbrookdale. A stroke of genius?

🔊 54

(1)Hardly. Economic historian Robert Allen points out that Darby's pivotal invention was a simple response to economic incentives. Existing iron smelters* used wood; it did not need an Einstein to think of chucking* coal in the furnace* instead. What it

10 required was a supply of the world's cheapest coal to make the project worthwhile, and that is exactly what Coalbrookdale's mines provided. Once he worked out that the economics were viable, Darby simply commissioned researchers to experiment, solve the technical problems, and make (2)his project a reality. And even after Darby's invention was tried and tested, it did not spread to mainland Europe, for the simple

15 reason that Europe's coal was too expensive; most of it was shipped over from Newcastle in England anyway. Coke smelting in France or Germany was technologically possible, but just not profitable for 150 years.

🔊 55

This seems like an unusually straightforward case, but on closer inspection the same turns out to be true of many of the Industrial Revolution's technological advances.

20 Cotton-spinning machinery, for example, did not require any scientific knowledge, just a careful process of development and experimentation plus a little creativity: (3)legend has it that the spinning jenny* was inspired by a traditional medieval spinning wheel that fell over and kept spinning while lying on the ground. The inventors of spinning machines such as the spinning jenny and the water frame* launched serious research

25 programs; they knew exactly what they hoped to achieve, and just needed to solve a series of modest engineering problems.

🔊 56

(4)They expended this considerable effort rationally — and those in France or China rationally did not — because (5)the financials added up: Allen's calculations show that British workers were at that time the most highly paid in the world, whether

30 measured against the price of silver, of food, of energy, or of capital. That meant that they were big consumers of imported cotton, but also that a labour-saving device would pay dividends*. In Britain, a spinning jenny cost less than five months' wages, while in low-wage France it cost more than a year's wages. It was cheap French labour that accounted for the machine's slow adoption on the continent, not the superior scientific

35 ingenuity of the British.

57   That was even more true of steam engines. They were, unusually for Industrial Revolution technology, based on an actual scientific advance: Galileo discovered that atmosphere had weight and so could exert pressure. Yet the practical invention took place in Britain, not in Galileo's Italy, and again, the reason was not genius but the fact that labour was expensive and fuel was incredibly cheap. Allen calculates that, in terms 40 of thermal units* per hour, wages in Newcastle in those days were perhaps ten times higher than those in continental cities such as Paris and Strasbourg. Labour in China was even cheaper. By the same reckoning, London wages were three times higher than those in continental cities and six or seven times those in Beijing. (6)It's no surprise that the steam engine, a device for replacing labour with coal, was a British invention. 45

58   All this shows that many of the important innovations of the Industrial Revolution were calculated and deliberate responses to high British wages and cheap British coal. The cheap coal was an accident of geography, but the wages weren't. Our historical detective story leads us to another question: (7)—————————————

  *   Coalbrookdale イングランド西部の地名   smelter「精錬所」   chuck「投げる」   furnace「炉」
     spinning jenny「ジェニー紡績機」   water frame「水力紡績機」   pay dividends「後で元がとれる」
     thermal unit「熱量単位」

解答欄

                                                 10   20

1

2

3

4

5

                                                 10   20

6

7

8

| 語句 | 音声は、「英語」→「日本語の意味」の順で読まれます。 | CD 1- Tr 59-62 |

1	with ... in mind	
2	in the form of …	
7	hardly [hάrdli]	
18	unusually [ʌnjúːʒuəli]	
23	inventor [invéntər]	
28	calculation [kὰlkjəléiʃən]	
38	atmosphere [ǽtməsfìər]	
45	invention [invénʃən]	

入試標準レベル（共通テスト・私大）

4	not to mention …	
10	worthwhile [wə́rðhwáil]	
11	mine [máin] （名）	
17	profitable [prάfitəbəl]	
19	be true of …	
21	creativity [krìːeitívəti]	
22	medieval [mìːdíːvəl]	
23	fall over	
24	launch [lɔ́ntʃ] （動）	
26	modest [mάdəst]	
27	considerable [kənsídərəbl]	
30	measure A against B	
31	device [diváis]	
32	wage [wéidʒ]	
34	account for …	
34	adoption [ədάpʃən]	
38	practical [prǽktikəl]	
40	incredibly [inkrédəbli]	
40	calculate [kǽlkjəlèit]	
40	in terms of …	
42	continental [kὰntənéntəl]	
47	calculated [kǽlkjulèitəd]	

入試発展レベル（二次・有名私大）

8	incentive [inséntiv]	
15	ship [ʃíp] （動）	
27	rationally [rǽʃənəli]	
28	add up	

38	exert [igzə́rt]	
46	innovation [ìnəvéiʃən]	
47	deliberate [dilíbərət] （形）	

その他

2	coke [kóuk]	コークス
2	foundational [faundéiʃənəl]	基礎をなす、基本の
3	the Industrial Revolution	産業革命
4	steamship [stíːmʃìp]	蒸気船
4	industrial machinery	産業機械
5	a stroke of genius	天才的なひらめき
7	pivotal [pívətəl]	極めて重要な、中枢の
11	work out that …	…だと理解する
12	economics [èːkənάmiks]	経済状態、経済学
12	viable [váiəbl]	実行可能な
12	commission … to do	…に～するよう委任する
18	straightforward [strèitfɔ́rwərd]	直接的な、わかりやすい
20	cotton-spinning machinery	綿紡績機
21	experimentation [ikspèrimentéiʃən]	実験
21	legend has it that …	伝説によれば…である
22	spinning wheel	糸車、紡ぎ車
23	spin [spín] （動）	高速にくるくる回転する、糸を紡ぐ
26	engineering problem	技術的課題
27	expend [ikspénd]	費やす、消費する
28	financials [fənǽnʃəlz]	〔複数形で〕財源、収入、財政状態
30	capital [kǽpətəl] （名）	元金、資本
35	ingenuity [ìndʒənúːəti]	発明の才、独創性
43	reckoning [rékəniŋ]	計算、見積もり

展開	段落	要旨
序論	1	ダービーは（①　　　　　　）を燃料に安価な（②　　　　　　）生産に成功して（③　　　　　　）の基礎を築いたが、これは天才のなせる業だったのか？
主題の展開①	2	経済的誘因に反応したにすぎず、世界一安価な（①　　　　　　）供給が可能にした発明だ、とアレンは指摘する。（①　　　　　　）が高すぎた（④　　　　　　　）大陸には、新技術は広がらなかった。
主題の展開②	3	同様なことは（③　　　　　　）の多くの技術的進歩に当てはまり、必要なのは（⑤　　　　　　）知識ではなく、入念な開発・実験過程、多少の創造力だけだった。
主題の展開③	4	（⑥　　　　　　）が技術開発の努力を進めたのは（⑤　　　　　　）才能が優れていたからではなく、採算が合ったからで、その一因は労働者の世界一の（⑦　　　　　　）にあった。
主題の展開④	5	蒸気機関の実用的な発明も（⑥　　　　　　）でなされたが、この理由も天賦の才ではなく、労働者の（⑦　　　　　　）と極めて安価な燃料にあった。
結論	6	（③　　　　　　）の重要な革新的技術は、（⑥　　　　　　）の（⑦　　　　　　）と安価な（①　　　　　　）に対する計算された反応だった。

（下書き）

									10										20

									10										20

本文解説

❶ 【分詞構文】【not to mention ...】

(l.2) His success was foundational to the Industrial Revolution, **allowing** the production of less expensive iron and so **enabling** the construction of railways, steamships and industrial machinery, **not to mention** the famous iron bridge built by Darby's grandson near Coalbrookdale.

- ▶ allowing と enabling の 2 つで分詞構文を作り、and so で結ばれている。and so は allowing ... iron を受け「だから、それゆえ」の意味。両者とも意味上の主語は主節の主語 His success なので、His success allowed the production of less expensive iron and so (it) enabled the construction of ... と読む。用法は、彼の成功が産業革命の基盤となった原因・理由、あるいは彼の成功が産業革命の基盤となった具体的内容の説明、いずれとも解釈できる。
- ▶ not to mention ... は「…は言うまでもなく」の意味。

❷ 【省略】【measured against ...】

(l.28) Allen's calculations show that British workers were at that time the most highly paid in the world, **whether measured against** the price of silver, of food, of energy, **or** of capital.

- ▶ whether A or B「A であろうと B であろうと」省略を補うと、whether (their wages were) measured against the price of silver, of food, of energy, or (they were measured against the price) of capital となる。of はすべて the price に続く。 measure A against B「A を B と比較する」

❸ 【強調構文】【account for ...】

(l.33) **It was** cheap French labour **that accounted for** the machine's slow adoption on the continent, not the superior scientific ingenuity of the British.

- ▶ It was 〜 that ... の形の強調構文。「the superior scientific ingenuity of the British ではなく cheap French labour こそ…だった」と二者を対比している点にも注意。
- ▶ account for ...「(事が) …の原因を説明する (=explain)、…の主な原因となる」
  ex. Recent pressure of work may account for his behavior this time.
  「最近の仕事のストレスが彼の今回の行動の原因だろう」

❹ 【for の意味】

(l.36) That was even more true of steam engines. They were, unusually **for** Industrial Revolution technology, based on an actual scientific advance:

- ▶ この for は「…にしては」の意味。英英辞典に used to say a particular quality of someone or something is surprising when you consider what they are「人や物・事の特質が本来の姿と比べて意外なときに用いる」とある。
  ex. It was an unusually warm day for December.
  「12 月にしては珍しく暖かな日だった」
- ▶ unusually for Industrial Revolution technology「(蒸気機関は) 産業革命の技術としては珍しいことに」

(l.43) By the same reckoning, London wages were **three times higher than those** in continental cities and **six or seven times those** in Beijing.

▶ three times higher than those（=the wages）= three times as high as those(=the wages) 倍数表現としては〈X times as 原級 as ...〉があるが、〈X times 比較級 than ...〉もよく使われている。後者は「…より X 倍だけ〜」という加算の意味ではなく、前者と同意である。

▶ six or seven times those は、three times higher than those を受けた six or seven times（higher than）those の省略と見ることもできるが、この形の倍数表現〈X times 名詞（句）〉もよく使われる。

ex. Taro earns three times my salary.
「太郎は私の給料の 3 倍稼いでいる」

According to Shoshana Zuboff, a professor at the Harvard Business School, 🔊63
surveillance* capitalism originated with the brilliant discoveries and the bold and
shameless claims of one American firm: Google.

Incorporated in 1998, Google soon came to dominate Internet search. But initially, 🔊64
5 it did not focus on advertising and had no clear path to profitability. What it did have
was a completely new insight: the data it derived from searches — the numbers and
patterns of questions, their phrasing, people's click patterns, and so on — could be
used to improve Google's search results and add new services for users. This would
attract more users, which would in turn further improve its search engine in (1)a
10 repeating cycle of learning and expansion.

(2)Google's commercial breakthrough came in 2002, when it saw that it could also 🔊65
use the data it collected to profile the users themselves according to their characteristics
and interests. Then, instead of matching ads with search questions, the company could
match ads with individual users. Targeting ads precisely and efficiently to individuals
15 is the Holy Grail* of advertising. Rather than being Google's customers, Zuboff
argues, the users became its raw-material suppliers, from whom the firm derived what
she calls "behavioral surplus." That surplus consists of the data above and beyond
what Google needs to improve user services.

(3)Together with the company's formidable capabilities in artificial intelligence, 🔊66
20 Google's enormous flows of data enabled it to create what Zuboff sees as the true
basis of the surveillance industry — "prediction products," which anticipate what users
will do "now, soon, and later." Predicting what people will buy is the key to advertising,
but behavioral predictions have obvious value for other purposes, as well, such as
insurance, hiring decisions, and political campaigns.

25 Zuboff's analysis helps make sense of (4)the seemingly unrelated services offered 🔊67
by Google, its diverse ventures and many acquisitions. Gmail, Google Maps, the
Android operating system, YouTube, Google Home, even self-driving cars — these
and dozens of other services are all ways, Zuboff argues, of expanding the company's
"supply routes" for user data both on- and offline. Asking for permission to obtain
30 those data has not been part of the company's operating style. For instance, when the
company was developing Street View, a feature of its mapping service that displays
photographs of different locations, it went ahead and recorded images of streets and
homes in different countries without first asking for local permission, fighting off
opposition as it arose. In the surveillance business, any undefended area of social life
35 is (5)fair game.

68   This pattern of expansion reflects an underlying logic of the industry: in the competition for artificial intelligence and surveillance revenues, the advantage goes to the firms that can acquire both vast and varied streams of data. The other companies engaged in surveillance capitalism at the highest level — Amazon, Facebook, Microsoft, and the big telecommunications companies — also face the same expansionary needs.   40 Step by step, (6)the industry has expanded both the scope of surveillance (by migrating from the virtual into the real world) and the depth of surveillance (by going into the interiors of individuals' lives and accumulating data on their personalities, moods, and emotions).

*   surveillance：spying, observation
   Holy Grail：a thing which is eagerly pursued or sought after

解答欄

1
....
....

2
....
....

3
....
....
....

4
....
....

5
....

6
....
....
....

7
....

語句　音声は、「英語」→「日本語の意味」の順で読まれます。　CD 1- Tr 69-72

入試基礎レベル

13 **instead of ...**

14 **individual** [ìndəvídʒuəl]（形）

17 **consist of ...**

20 **flow** [flóu]（名）

21 **basis** [béisis]

24 **hiring** [háiəriŋ]

28 **expand** [ikspǽnd]

31 **feature** [fíːtʃər]（名）

31 **display** [displéi]（動）

36 **reflect** [riflékt]

37 **competition for ...**

38 **acquire** [əkwáiər]

38 **vast** [vǽst]

38 **varied** [véərid]（形）

入試標準レベル（共通テスト・私大）

2 **originate with ...**

4 **dominate** [dámənèit]

4 **initially** [iníʃəli]

5 **advertising** [ǽdvərtàiziŋ]

5 **path to ...**

6 **insight** [ínsàit]

6 **derive A from B**

9 **in turn**

10 **expansion** [ikspǽnʃən]

11 **commercial** [kəmə́ːrʃəl]

12 **characteristic** [kæ̀rəktərístik]

13 **match A with B**

14 **target A to B**

16 **raw-material**

19 **together with ...**

19 **capability** [kèipəbíləti]

19 **artificial intelligence**

20 **enormous** [inɔ́ːrməs]

21 **prediction** [pridíkʃən]

24 **insurance** [inʃúərəns]

24 **political campaign**

25 **make sense of ...**

25 **seemingly** [síːmiŋli]

26 **diverse** [daivə́ːrs]

29 **permission** [pərmíʃən]

29 **obtain** [əbtéin]

33 **fight off ...**

34 **opposition** [àpəzíʃən]

36 **underlying** [ʌ̀ndərláiiŋ]（形）

36 **logic** [ládʒik]

39 **(be) engaged in ...**

42 **depth** [dépθ]

43 **interior** [intíəriər]（名）

43 **personality** [pə̀ːrsənǽləti]

入試発展レベル（二次・有名私大）

2 **bold** [bóuld]

5 **profitability** [prɑ̀fətəbíləti]

11 **breakthrough** [bréikθrùː]

17 **behavioral** [bihéivjərəl]

17 **surplus** [sə́ːrplʌs]

21 **anticipate** [æntísəpèit]

26 **acquisition** [æ̀kwizíʃən]

27 **self-driving car**

34 **arise** [əráiz]

34 **undefended** [ʌ̀ndiféndid]（形）

38 **stream** [stríːm]

40 **expansionary** [ikspǽnʃənèri]（形）

41 **scope** [skóup]（名）

41 **migrate from A into B**

42 **virtual** [və́ːrtʃuəl]

43 **accumulate** [əkjúːmjəlèit]

2 **surveillance** [sərvéiləns] 監視、見張り

2 **capitalism** [kǽpitəlìzm] 資本主義

4 **incorporate** [inkɔ́ːrpərèit]

法人 [会社] 組織にする

7 **phrasing** [fréiziŋ] 言葉遣い、言い回し

7 **click** [klík]

(マウスの操作での) クリック

12 **profile** [próufail]（動）

(情報に基づき顧客などの人物像や行動を) 予測する

15 **the Holy Grail**

達成困難な目標、究極の理想

19 **formidable** [fɔ́ːrmidəbl]

圧倒的な、恐ろしいほどの、大変な

26 **venture** [véntʃər] ベンチャー企業、新興企業

29 **online** [ànláin]

オンラインで [の]、ネットワーク上で [の]

29 **offline** [ɔ̀ːfláin]

オフラインで [の]、ネットワークに接続しない (で)

30 **operating style** 営業スタイル

31 **mapping service** 地図サービス

35 **fair game**

(批判・攻撃などの) かっこうの的

37 **revenue** [révənjùː] 収益、収入

40 **telecommunication** [tèləkəmjuːnəkéiʃən]

電気通信、遠距離通信

段落要旨　　各段落のまとめとなるように、空所に適切な語句を入れなさい。（同じ番号には、同じ語句が入ります）

展開	段落	要旨
主題の提示	1	（①　　　　　　　　　　）は、グーグルの優れた発見と大胆で恥知らずの主張から始まった。
主題の展開①	2	グーグルは、インターネット検索で得た（②　　　　　　）が、検索の質の向上と新サービスの追加に利用できると考えていた。
主題の展開②	3	グーグルは、ユーザーのデータを利用し、（③　　　　　）を個々のユーザーに合わせることにより商業面で躍進した。グーグルにとって、ユーザーは原材料を供給する存在になり、サービス向上に必要とする以上のデータを得た。
主題の展開③	4	グーグルは人工知能と膨大なデータを利用し、ユーザーの行動を（④　　　　　　　　　）するという、監視産業の基盤を作り出した。
主題の展開④	5	グーグルの多様なサービスは、データ収集の供給ルートを拡大するための手段であり、収集は許可なく行われた。監視ビジネスでは、社会生活の無防備な領域も監視の標的となる。
結論	6	監視産業では、膨大で多様なデータの流れを獲得できる企業が有利である。この業界は、現実世界での監視範囲と、（⑤　　　　　　　　　）の内部へ入り込むことによる監視の深度を拡大している。

百字要約　　「段落要旨」を参考にして、本文全体の内容を百字程度の日本語で要約しなさい。

（下書き）

									10										20

									10										20

Memo

本文解説

❶ 【受動態の分詞構文】

(l.4) **Incorporated** in 1998, Google soon came to dominate Internet search.

▶ Incorporated in 1998 は過去分詞で始まる受動態の分詞構文で、過去分詞の前に Being が省略されている。意味上の主語は主節の主語の Google、また主節は過去形で書かれているので、文にすると Google was incorporated in 1998 となる。分詞構文は、分詞で始まる句が副詞の働きをして、文に情報を加えるものなので、「1998 年に法人化されたグーグルは、すぐに〜した」といった意味になる。

▶ being で始まる分詞構文では、その being が省略されることが多い。また、位置は文頭、文末が多いが、文中のこともある。

ex. Persuaded by his friends, Brutus decided to kill Caesar.
「友人たちに説得されて、ブルータスはシーザーを殺そうと決心した」
The engineers, sometimes discouraged, were confident of the success of a new product development.
「技術者たちは、時に落ち込むことはあったが、新製品の開発の成功には自信があった」
The student entered the room, accompanied by his parents.
「その生徒は両親に付き添われて部屋に入った」

❷ 【非制限用法［継続用法］の関係副詞】

(l.11) Google's commercial breakthrough came in 2002, **when** it saw that it could also use the data it collected to profile the users themselves according to their characteristics and interests.

▶ when ... は関係副詞の非制限用法［継続用法］で、when の前にコンマ (,) が置かれている。直前の 2002（= the year 2002）を受け、それについて「そしてその年にグーグルは〜とわかった」と追加の説明を加えている。

▶ 関係副詞の when と where には非制限用法［継続用法］があり、それぞれ「そしてそのとき〜 (= and then 〜)」、「そしてその場所で〜 (= and there 〜)」などの意味を表す。先行詞は、特定の時、場所のことが多く、特に固有名詞は非制限用法［継続用法］の関係詞節が続くのが普通である。

ex. Wait till Sunday, when I will tell you everything about the matter.
「日曜日まで待ってください。そのときに、その件についてすべてお話しします」
Hameln, where he was born and brought up, is famous for the folk tale of "The Pied Piper of Hamelin".
「彼が生まれ育ったハーメルンは、『ハーメルンの笛吹き男』の民話で有名だ」

(l.15) Rather than being Google's customers, Zuboff argues, the users became its raw-material suppliers**, from whom** the firm derived what she calls "behavioral surplus."

> ▶ from whom ... は〈前置詞＋関係代名詞〉の非制限用法［継続用法］で、from whom の前にコンマ（,）が置かれている。関係代名詞 whom は直前の its raw-material suppliers を受け、「そしてその原材料供給者から、会社（＝グーグル社）は〜を得た」と追加の説明を加えている。and from its raw-material suppliers the firm derived ... の意味である。

> ▶ 〈前置詞＋関係代名詞〉の用法では、先行詞が人の場合は〈前置詞＋ whom〉が、人以外の場合は〈前置詞＋ which〉が使われる。

> *ex.* When I studied in Canada, I made many friends, with whom I shared not only lessons but also invaluable experiences.
> 「カナダ留学中、私は多くの友人を得たが、彼らとは授業だけでなく、かけがえのない経験をともにした」
> I think most people have heard of "the lost city of Atlantis," about which many books have been written.
> 「大多数の人が『失われた都市アトランティス』については聞いたことがあると思います。それについては多くの本が書かれていますから」

4 【the key to ...】【as well】【such as ...】

(l.22) Predicting what people will buy is **the key to** advertising, but behavioral predictions have obvious value for other purposes, **as well**, **such as** insurance, hiring decisions, and political campaigns.

> ▶「…（へ）の鍵、秘けつ、手がかり」は、英語では the spare key to his house「彼の家の合い鍵（スペアキー）」、the key to success「成功への鍵［秘けつ］」、the key to (solving) the problem「その問題を解く鍵［手がかり］」のように、the key of ... ではなく、the key to ... で表現する。

> ▶ as well は「〜もまた、同様に」の意味。文末に置かれるので、何と同様なのかは文脈から判断する必要がある。この文では「behavioral predictions が advertising だけでなく other purposes にも価値を持つ」の意味で、other purposes の後に such as ... と続き、その例が挙げられている。such as ... は「…のような」の意味で、具体例を列挙するときに用いられる。

5 【文構造】【all の用法】

(l.26) Gmail, Google Maps, the Android operating system, YouTube, Google Home, even self-driving cars — these and dozens of other services are **all** ways, **Zuboff argues**, of expanding the company's "supply routes" for user data both on- and offline.

> ▶ ダッシュ（—）以下では、まず前の6つの項目 Gmail ... self-driving cars をまとめて these と言い直し、それと dozens of other services が are の主語（S）になっている。Zuboff argues が途中に挿入されているが、Zuboff argues that Gmail, Google Maps ... cars are all ways of expanding .... と読む。

> ▶〈ways of *doing*〉で「〜する方法［手段］」。S are all ways of ... の all は S と〈同格〉の代名詞で、「S はどれもすべて、…する手段だ」の意味。「S は…するすべての手段だ」ではない。

> *ex.* A few people have remained in the village, but the others have all gone to town.
> 「村に残った人も少数いるが、その他の人たちはみんな都会に行ってしまった」

九州大学　472 words

CD 2

🔊1

The concept of altruism is ready for retirement.

Not that the phenomenon of helping others and doing good to other people is about to go away — not at all. On the contrary, the appreciation of the importance of bonds between individuals is on the rise in the modern understanding of animal and
5 human societies. What needs to go away is the basic idea behind the concept of altruism — that there is a conflict of interest between helping yourself and helping others.

The word "altruism" was coined in the 1850s by the great French sociologist 🔊2 Auguste Comte. What it means is that you do something for other people (the Old
10 French *altrui*, from the Latin *alter*), not just for yourself. Thus, it opposes egoism or selfishness. (1)<u>This concept is rooted in the notion that human beings and animals are dominated by selfishness and egoism, so that you need a concept to explain why they sometimes behave unselfishly and kindly to others.</u>

But the reality is different: Humans are deeply bound to other humans, and most 🔊3
15 actions are reciprocal and in the interest of both (2)<u>parties</u> (or, in the case of hatred, in the disinterest of both). The starting point is neither selfishness nor altruism but the state of being bound together. It's an illusion to believe that you can be happy when no one else is. Or that other people will not be affected by your unhappiness.

Behavioral science and neurobiology have shown how intimately we're bound. 🔊4
20 Phenomena like mimicry⋆, emotional contagion⋆, empathy, sympathy, compassion, and prosocial⋆ behavior are evident in humans and animals alike. (3)<u>We're influenced by the well-being of others in more ways than we normally care to think of.</u> Therefore, a simple rule applies: *Everyone feels better when you're well, and you feel better when everyone is well.*

25 This correlated state is the real one. Egoism and its opposite concept, altruism, are 🔊5 unsubstantial concepts — shadows or even illusions. This applies also to the immediate psychological level: If helping others fills you with satisfaction, is it not also in your own interest to help others? Are you not, then, helping yourself? Being kind to others means being (ア).

30 Likewise, if you feel better and make more money when you're generous and 🔊6 contribute to the well-being and resources of other people — as in the welfare societies

that, like Scandinavian countries, became rich through sharing and equality — then whoever wants to keep everything for himself or herself, with no gift-giving, no taxpaying, and no generosity, is just an amateur egoist. (4)Real egoists share.

It's not altruistic to be an altruist — just wise. Helping others is in your own interest. We don't need a concept to explain that behavior. Auguste Comte's concept is therefore ready for retirement. We can all just help each other, without wondering why.

35

* mimicry : the activity or art of copying the behavior or speech of other people
  contagion : the spreading of something bad from person to person
  prosocial : helpful and beneficial for other people and society

解答欄

1

10   20

2

3

4

5

6

7

| 語句 | 音声は、「英語」→「日本語の意味」の順で読まれます。 | CD 2- Tr 8-11 |

1　be ready for ～

2　not that ...

10　oppose [əpóuz]

17　state [stéit]（名）

26　immediate [imíːdiət]

1　concept [kάnsèpt]（名）

1　retirement [ritáiərmənt]（名）

2　phenomenon [fənάmənən]

2　do good to ～

2　be about to *do*

3　on the contrary

3　appreciation [əprìːʃiéiʃən]

4　bond [bάnd]（名）

6　conflict [kάnflikt]（名）

11　notion [nóuʃən]

14　bind A to B

15　in the case of ～

15　hatred [héitrid]

17　illusion [ilúːʒən]

19　intimately [íntəmətli]

20　sympathy [símpəθi]

21　evident [évidənt]

21　A and B alike

22　well-being [wélbìiŋ]

26　apply to ～

30　likewise [láikwàiz]

31　contribute to ～

34　generosity [dʒènərάsəti]

34　amateur [ǽmətʃùər]（形）

4　on the rise

6　interest [íntərəst]（名）　利害

8　sociologist [sòusiάlədʒist]

10　Latin [lǽtn]（名）

10　egoism [íːgouìzəm]

11　selfishness [sélfiʃnəs]

11　be rooted in ～

13　unselfishly [ʌnsélfiʃli]

15　in the interest of ～　～の利益にかなって

15　party [pάrti]（名）

16　disinterest [disíntərəst]

20　compassion [kəmpǽʃən]

22　care to *do*

26　unsubstantial [ʌnsəbstǽnʃəl]

33　keep ～ for *oneself*

33　gift-giving

34　taxpaying [tǽkspèiiŋ]

34　egoist [íːgouist]

1　altruism [ǽltruìzm]　利他主義、利他的行為

8　coin [kɔ́in]（動）　（新語などを）造り出す

9　Auguste Conte　オーギュスト・コント

9　Old French　古フランス語

15　reciprocal [risíprəkəl]　相互的な、互恵的な

19　behavioral science　行動科学

19　neurobiology [njùroubaiάlədʒi]　神経生物学

20　mimicry [mímikri]　模倣、まね

20　contagion [kəntéidʒən]　伝染、感化

20　empathy [émpəθi]　共感、感情移入

21　prosocial [prəusóuʃəl]　向社会的な、社会性のある

25　correlated [kɔ́ːrilèitid]　相関的な

31　resources [ríːsɔ̀ːrsiz]　〔複数形で〕資産、財産

32　Scandinavian [skændənéiviən]　スカンジナビアの

35　altruistic [æltruístik]　利他的な

35　altruist [ǽltruːist]　利他主義者

展開	段落	要旨
主題の提示 (結論)	1	(①　　　　　　) 主義は引退の準備ができている。
主題の展開 ①	2	引退すべきは (①　　　　　　) 主義の概念の背後にある、「自分を助けることと他者を助けることの間には (②　　　　　　) の対立がある」という考えだ。
主題の展開 ②	3	altruism は (③　　　　　) による造語で、利己主義と対立する概念だ。これは、人間が時折他人に優しく振る舞う理由を説明するための概念である。
主題の展開 ③	4	現実は自分本位も (①　　　　　) 主義もなく、人間は互いに深く結ばれているというのが原点だ。ほとんどの行動は (④　　　　　) 的で、双方の利益にかなっている。
主題の展開 ④	5	人間が互いに密接に結ばれていることは、科学的にも明らかにされている。我々は他人の (⑤　　　　　) に大いに影響を受けているのだ。
主題の展開 ⑤	6	そのような共に結ばれている相関的状態は現実である一方で、利己主義と (①　　　　　　) 主義は実体のない概念、つまり (⑥　　　　　) だ。
主題の展開 ⑥	7	他人の (⑤　　　　　) や資産に気前よく貢献することで、自分もいっそう気分よく感じ、多くのお金も得られるのだから、真の利己主義者は分け合う。
結論	8	(①　　　　　　) 主義者であることは (①　　　　　　) 的を意味しない。他人を助けることは自分の利益になるので、その行為を説明するための概念は必要ない。

(下書き)　　　　　　　　　　　　　　　　　　　　　　　10　　　　　　　　　　　　　　　　　　　　20

（解答欄の原稿用紙マス目）

10　　　　　　　　　　　　　　　　　　　　20

（解答欄の原稿用紙マス目）

本文解説

1 【not that ～】【not at all】

(l.2) (The concept of altruism is ready for retirement.) **Not that** the phenomenon of helping others and doing good to other people is about to go away — **not at all**.

> ▶ この Not that ～は It is not that ～の省略で、that 節の内容を否定する。前文に対して「(だからといって)～というわけではない」の意味。ここでは「(利他主義という概念は引退の準備ができている。) だからといって、他人を助け、他人に対して善行をなすという現象が…というわけではない」。

> *ex.* He wouldn't tell me how much he paid for the yacht. Not that I was really interested.
> 「彼はそのヨットにいくら払ったか言おうとしなかった。もっとも、私が本当に興味があったわけではないが」

> *cf.* Not that I won't help you, of course, but I have little time.
> 「もちろん、君を手伝わないって言ってるんじゃない。ただ、時間があまりないんだ」

> ▶ not at all は、Not that ～という否定文の内容をさらに強く否定して、「全くそういうことではないのだ」の意味。

2 【in the interest of ...】【文構造】

(l.14) But the reality is different: Humans are deeply bound to other humans, and most actions are reciprocal and **in the interest of** both parties (or, **in the case of hatred, in the disinterest of** both).

> ▶ in the interest(s) of ... で「…の利益にかなって、…にとって有利な」。英英辞典では、If something is *in the interests of* a particular person or group, it will benefit them in some way. と説明されている。第6段落第3文後半の is it not also in your own interest to help others? の in *one's* (own) interest も同様の意味で、「他人を助けることは、あなた自身の利益にもなっていないだろうか?」。

> ▶ ここの party は、bound to other humans や most actions are reciprocal からも判断できるように、「(交渉・事件・契約などの) 当事者、関係者、相手」。

> ▶ or 以下は in the case of hatred, actions are in the disinterest of both parties を略したもので、直前の「行動が双方の利益になる」から判断すると、「互いに憎しみ合っている場合は、双方の不利益になる」の意味だろう。ただし、disinterest は通常「無関心 (= lack of interest; indifference)」あるいは「公平さ (= lack of personal or selfish interest)」の意味なので、この in the disinterest of both は "not in the interest of either" などとする方が正用法だろう。

(l.30) Likewise, **if** you feel better and make more money when you're generous and contribute to the well-being and resources of other people — as in the welfare societies that, like Scandinavian countries, became rich through sharing equality — **then whoever** wants to keep everything for himself or herself, with no gift-giving, no taxpaying, and no generosity, is just an amateur egoist.

▸ if で始まる従属節の最後に、as in the welfare societies ... equality「…の福祉社会におけるように」がダッシュ（—）にはさまれて挿入されている。

▸ then は if 節に呼応して「（もし〜ならば）そのときは、その場合は」の意味。この文のように if 節が長い場合は、主節をはっきりさせるためにも then を用いる方がよいとされる。

ex. If you feel ill, then you must stay home.
「気分が悪いなら家にいなさい」

▸ whoever は「〜する人はだれでも（= anyone[any people] who 〜）」を意味する複合関係代名詞。この文では whoever wants to ... no generosity,「…したい人はだれでも」までが主部。

ex. The store gave a small present to whoever visited it on the opening day.
「その店は開店日に訪れた人にはだれにでも、ちょっとしたプレゼントを配った」

Explaining the world through stories is, of course, nothing new. Stories and storytelling are as fundamental to human nature as science, and every culture we have records of has its creation story and tales of moral instruction. Although our detailed knowledge of ancient stories extends back only a few thousand years, to the beginnings of written language, human fascination with narrative most likely stretches back much further. Stone carvings and cave paintings dating back forty thousand years mix human and animal figures in interesting ways, and it's easy to imagine that there are stories behind the images.

Indeed, the tendency to seek and invent narrative is a deeply rooted part of human nature. We see stories everywhere we look. (A)In a classic psychology experiment, people asked to describe a short animation of geometric shapes moving about a screen used language that attributed intention to the shapes, as if the objects were conscious actors: "The red triangle chased the blue circle off the screen."

Young children live in a world with little distinction between fact and story. As I started writing this book, my four-year-old daughter was going through a superhero phase. At various times, she identified herself as Strong Girl, Fast Girl, Brave Girl, Smart Girl, Ninja Girl, and Butterfly Girl, and nearly every day, we heard a new story of how her heroic actions stopped the various Bad Guys. Now that she's older, her stories have become more and more involved and are a reliable source of parental entertainment.

This fascination with narrative carries over to explanations of how the world works.

(a) These stories generally seem peculiar and almost comical, as modern scientific explanations of weather in terms of the motion of air and water in the atmosphere are vastly more effective at predicting the course of major storms.

(b) A large chunk of mythology consists of attempts to impose narrative on the world, by attributing natural phenomena to capricious or revengeful gods and heroes.

(c) And yet, when a weather disaster does strike, it is virtually (and depressingly) certain that at least one fundamentalist religious leader will attribute it to divine vengeance for something or another.

Modern superstition operates on a smaller scale, as well. Every newspaper in America runs a daily horoscope column, which millions of people read and follow. Otherwise highly educated people will behave as if the motion of distant planets had some significant influence over chance events and interpersonal interactions on Earth.

(B)The stubborn persistence of even readily falsifiable ideas like astrology shows the power of the human desire to impose narrative on random events.

✎17   (C)Storytelling and even myth making have a place in science, too. In learning about physics, for example, a student can hardly avoid hearing the famous stories of Galileo Galilei's dropping weights off the Leaning Tower of Pisa and Isaac Newton's 40 inventing his theory of gravity when an apple fell on him. Of course, neither of these stories is literally true. There are elements of truth to both — Galileo did careful experiments to demonstrate that light and heavy objects fall at the same rate, and Newton did some of his critical work on gravitation at his family farm, while avoiding a plague outbreak in London. But the colorful and specific stories about the origins 45 of those theories are almost completely fiction. These persist, though, because they are useful. They help fix the key science in the minds of students by embedding the facts within a narrative. A disconnected series of abstract facts and figures is very difficult to remember, but if you can weave those facts into a story, they become easier to remember. The stories of Galileo in the tower and Newton under the apple 50 tree help bring home one of the key early ideas in physics by relying on the power of stories (in fact, most people remember the stories long after they've forgotten the underlying science).

✎18   Essentially all successful scientific theories contain an element of narrative: Event A leads to effect B, which explains observation C. (D)Some sciences even have to resist 55 the temptation to impose too much narrative: Evolutionary biologists have struggled for years against the notion that evolution is inherently progressive, working toward some kind of goal. And one of the serious errors of reporting on medical and psychological research is the mistaken assumption that when two phenomena tend to occur together, one phenomenon must cause the other. "Correlation is not 60 causation" is a slogan among scientists and doubters, for good reason.

解答欄

1

....

....

....

....

2

....

次ページへ続く→

9.

3
....
....
....

4
....
....
....
....

5
....
....
....
....

6
....

語句　音声は、「英語」→「日本語の意味」の順で読まれます。　　　　CD 2- Tr 19-22

入試基礎レベル

13 **conscious** [kánʃəs] ....
13 **actor** [ǽktər] ....
42 **element** [éləmənt] ....
45 **origin** [ɔ́rədʒin] ....

入試標準レベル（共通テスト・私大）

3 **detailed** [ditéild]（形）.....................
10 **classic** [klǽsik] ....
12 **attribute A to B** ....
12 **intention** [inténʃən] ....
24 **motion** [móuʃən] ....
25 **vastly** [vǽstli] ....
29 **virtually** [vɔ́:rtʃuəli] ....
32 **operate** [ápərèit] ....
36 **readily** [rédili] ....
38 **myth** [míθ] ....
41 **gravity** [grǽvəti] ....
42 **literally** [lítərəli] ....
44 **critical** [krítikəl] ....
48 **a series of ...** ....
48 **abstract** [ǽbstrækt]（形）.....................
57 **progressive** [prəgrésiv] ....
59 **assumption** [əsʌ́mpʃən] ....

5	**fascination with ...**	
5	**narrative** [nǽrətiv]	
5	**stretch back**	
6	**carving** [kárviŋ]（名）	
9	**rooted** [rúːtəd]（形）	
11	**geometric** [dʒìːəmétrik]	
11	**move about**	
13	**chase A off B**	
16	**identify oneself as ...**	
18	**heroic** [hiróuik]	
19	**involved** [inválvd]（形）複雑な、込み入った	
19	**parental** [pəréntəl]	
21	**carry over to ...**	
26	**a large chunk of ...**	
26	**mythology** [miθálədʒi]	
30	**divine** [diváin]	
32	**superstition** [sùːpərstíʃən]	
35	**interaction** [ìntərǽkʃən]	
36	**stubborn** [stʌ́bərn]	
36	**persistence** [pərsístəns]	
38	**have a place in ...** ...に位置を占める、...に存在する	
44	**gravitation** [grævitéiʃən]	
46	**persist** [pərsíst]（動）	
47	**embed** [imbéd]	
53	**underlying** [ʌ́ndərlàiiŋ]（形）	
56	**temptation** [temptéiʃən]	
56	**struggle against ...**	
57	**inherently** [inhíərəntli]	

2	**storytelling** [stɔ́ːritèliŋ]	物語を語ること
3	**creation story**	創造物語
3	**moral instruction**	道徳教育
4	**extend back to ...**	...まで遡る
6	**cave painting**	洞窟壁画
25	**major storm**	大嵐
27	**capricious** [kəpríʃəs]	気まぐれな
27	**revengeful** [rivéndʒful]	執念深い、復讐心のある
29	**depressingly** [diprésiŋli] 気がめいるほど	
30	**fundamentalist** [fʌ̀ndəméntəlist] 原理主義者（の）	
31	**vengeance for ...**	...への復讐、報復
33	**run** [rʌn]	～を載せる
33	**horoscope** [hɔ́rəskòup]	星占い
35	**interpersonal** [ìntərpɔ́ːrsənəl] 個人間の、人間関係の	
36	**falsifiable** [fɔ́lsəfàiəbəl]	反証可能な
36	**astrology** [əstrálədʒi]	占星術
40	**the Leaning Tower of Pisa** ピサの斜塔	
48	**disconnected** [dìskənéktəd]（形）切れ切れの、一貫性のない	
49	**weave A into B**	A を織り交ぜて B を作る
51	**bring home ...**	...を十分に理解させる
56	**evolutionary biologist** 進化生物学者	
60	**correlation** [kɔ̀rəléiʃən]	相互関係、相関関係
61	**causation** [kɔzéiʃən]	因果関係
61	**doubter** [dáutər]	疑い深い人

9.

段落要旨　　各段落のまとめとなるように、空所に適切な語句を入れなさい。（同じ番号には、同じ語句が入ります）

展開	段落	要旨
主題の提示	1	（①　　　　　）を語ることは人間の本性にとって根源的なもので、人間が（①　　　　　）に魅了されたのは（②　　　　　）が生まれるよりはるか昔に遡るだろう。
主題の展開①	2	（③　　　　　）の実験で図形が動く動画の説明を求められた人々は、その図形に意志があるかのような言葉を使った（①　　　　　）で説明した。
主題の展開②	3	幼い子どもは（④　　　　　）と（①　　　　　）の区別がほとんどない世界に住んでおり、筆者の娘も自分をヒーローと同一視した英雄物語で親を喜ばせている。
主題の展開③	4	神話では（⑤　　　　　）を神や英雄の行為のせいにしたりするが、そうした（①　　　　　）を世界に押しつけようとする試みは現代においても見られる。
主題の展開④	5	現代でも（⑥　　　　　）を信じ、それに基づいて行動する人が多いが、これは偶発的な出来事に（①　　　　　）を押しつけたいという人間の願望の強さを示している。
主題の展開⑤	6	科学上の発見などに関する（①　　　　　）が、たとえ創作であっても存続しているのは、科学の重要な要素や（⑦　　　　　）な事実や数を、学生の頭に定着させるのに有用だからである。
主題の展開⑥	7	成功した科学理論はどれも（①　　　　　）の要素を含んでいるが、それが（⑧　　　　　）関係を（⑨　　　　　）関係だと思い込む誤りにつながる危険性もある。

百字要約　　「段落要旨」を参考にして、本文全体の内容を百字程度の日本語で要約しなさい。

（下書き）

Memo

本文解説

1 【関係代名詞の省略】

(l.1) Stories and storytelling are as fundamental to human nature as science, and every culture **we have records of** has its creation story and tales of moral instruction.

▶ every culture で始まる後半部の主部は every culture we have records of、述語動詞は has。every culture we have records of は every culture that[which] we have records の意味で、目的格の関係代名詞が省略された形。we have records of every culture「我々はどの文化の記録も持っている」→ every culture we have records of「記録を持つどんな文化も」のように、基になる文を作ってみるとわかりやすい。〈前置詞 +which〉を使って every culture of which we have records とも書ける。

ex. I'm interested in questions we have no answers for.
「私は我々が答えを持っていない疑問に興味がある」(← we have no answers for the questions)

2 【文構造】【attribute A to B】

(l.10) In a classic psychology experiment, / (S)people / asked to describe a short animation of geometric shapes moving about a screen (V)used (O)language / (関係代名詞節) that **attributed** intention **to** the shapes, / as if the objects were conscious actors : / "The red triangle chased the blue circle off the screen."

▶ people asked to ... about a screen が全体の主部、述語動詞は used、language がその目的語。that 以下の関係代名詞節は language を修飾している。

▶ asked to ... a screen は主語 people を修飾する過去分詞句。be asked to *do*「〜することを求められる」。a short animation of geometric shapes moving about a screen の of 以下は〈of + 意味上の主語 + 動名詞〉の形で、「幾何学的な図形が画面を動き回っている」の意味。

▶ attribute A to B は「A(性質など)が B に備わっていると考える」。used language that attributed intention to the shapes「図形に意志があると考えた言葉を用いた」とは、as if 〜「まるで〜かのように」以下の具体例から判断して、「動画を説明するように求められた人々が、その幾何学的な図形に意志があると思わせるような表現をした」ということ。

3 【run の用法】【継続用法の関係代名詞】

(l.32) Every newspaper in America **runs** a daily horoscope column**, which** millions of people read and follow.

▶ runs a daily horoscope column の run は、「(新聞などが)(記事や広告など)を載せる、掲載する」の意味で使われている。

ex. The popular dailies ran the story for weeks.
「大衆紙は何週間もその記事を載せた」

▶ which の先行詞は a daily horoscope column だが、直前にコンマがある継続用法。全体で Every newspaper in America runs a daily horoscope column, and millions of people read and follow the horoscope の意味。

4 【otherwise の用法】

(l.34) **Otherwise** highly educated people will behave as if the motion of distant planets had some significant influence over chance events and interpersonal interactions on Earth.

▶ この otherwise は副詞で「その他の点[面]では (= in every other respect)」の意味。highly educated「教養の高い」を修飾し、otherwise highly educated people で「その他の点では非常に教養の高い人々」。一般的な状況や性質に対してその「例外」に言及する用法で、ここでは「本来なら教養ある人々で、（前文にある）星占いを読み、それに従うとは考えられない人々なのだが」という意味が込められている。

ex. Irresolution is a defect in his otherwise perfect character.
「（優柔不断が、彼の、その他の点では完璧な性格の欠点だ→）彼は優柔不断なのが玉にきずだ」

5 【help の用法】【bring home ...】

(l.47) They(= the colorful and specific stories about the origins of those theories) **help fix** the key science in the minds of students by embedding the facts within a narrative.

(l.50) The stories of Galileo in the tower and Newton under the apple tree **help bring home** one of the key early ideas in physics by relying on the power of stories (in fact, most people remember the stories long after they've forgotten the underlying science).

▶ 上記の help は直後に動詞の原形 fix, bring が続き、「（物・事が）（〜するのに）役立つ、助けとなる」の意味で、この例のように〈help *do*〉の形、あるいは〈help to *do*〉の形をとる。「その物語は幼児が他人の感情を理解するのに役立つ」を表現するときは、The story helps young children (to) understand the feelings of other people. のように〈help ＋目的語＋ (to) *do*〉の形をとる。

▶ bring home (to B) A あるいは bring A home (to B) の形で、「A（事）を（B（人）に）十分に［正しく］理解させる (= make B understand how important or serious A is)」の意味。上記の文では A に当たる one of the key early ideas in physics がやや長い句なので、前者の形になっている。help bring home one of the key early ideas in physics で「物理学における重要な初期の概念を頭にたたき込むのに役立つ」。

ex. The results of the exams brought home to me how little I had learned.
「テストの結果を見て、自分がいかに勉強していなかったかを痛感した」

6 【同格節を導く that】【分詞構文】

(l.56) Evolutionary biologists have struggled for years against **the notion that** evolution is inherently progressive, **working** toward some kind of goal.

(l.58) And one of the serious errors of reporting on medical and psychological research is **the mistaken assumption that** when two phenomena tend to occur together, one phenomenon must cause the other.

▶ 第 1 文の the notion that 〜は、that 以下が the notion の同格節で「〜という概念」の意味。working toward some kind of goal は分詞構文で、その意味上の主語は evolution。evolution is inherently progressive, working toward some kind of goal で「進化は本質的に先へ進むもので、何らかの目的に向かって進んでいる」。

▶ 第 2 文の the mistaken assumption that 〜も同様に、that 以下が the mistaken assumption の同格節で「〜という誤った思い込み」の意味。that 以下には〈when S' + V'..., S + V 〜〉の形の複文が置かれている。

Why have social anxieties increased so dramatically in many developed countries ❀23 over the last half century, as one American psychologist's studies suggest they have? Why does the 'social evaluative threat' seem so great? (1)<u>A reasonable explanation is the break-up of the settled communities of the past.</u> People used to grow up knowing,
5 and being known by, many of the same people all their lives. Although geographical mobility had been increasing for several generations, the last half century has seen a particularly rapid rise.

At the beginning of this period it was still common for people — in rural and ❀24 urban areas alike — never to have travelled much beyond the boundaries of their
10 immediate city or village community. Married brothers and sisters, parents and grandparents, tended to remain living nearby and the community consisted of people who had often known each other for much of their lives. But now that so many people move from where they grew up, knowledge of neighbours tends to be superficial or non-existent. People's sense of identity used to be rooted in the community to
15 which they belonged, in people's real knowledge of each other, but now it is lost in the facelessness of mass society. Familiar faces have been replaced by a constant flow of strangers. As a result, who we are, identity itself, is endlessly open to question.

The problem is shown even in the difficulty we have in distinguishing between the ❀25 concept of the 'esteem' in which we may or may not be held by others, and our own
20 self-esteem. The evidence of our sensitivity to '(2)<u>social evaluative threat</u>', coupled with the American psychologist's evidence of long-term rises in anxiety, suggests that we may — by the standards of any previous society — have become highly self-conscious, overly concerned with how we appear to others, worried that we might come across as unattractive, boring, ignorant or whatever, and constantly trying to
25 manage the impressions we make. And at the core of our interactions with strangers is our concern at the social judgements and evaluations they might make: how do they rate us, did we give a good account of ourselves? This insecurity is part of the modern psychological condition.

Greater (3) between people seems to heighten their social evaluation anxieties ❀26
30 by increasing the importance of social status. Instead of accepting each other as equals on the basis of our common humanity as we might in more equal settings,

measuring each other's worth becomes more important as status differences widen. We come to see social position as a more important feature of a person's identity. Between strangers $_{(4)}$it may often be the main feature. As Ralph Waldo Emerson, the nineteenth-century American philosopher, said, 'It is very certain that each man 35 carries in his eye the exact indication of his rank in the immense scale of men, and we are always learning to read $_{(5)}$it.' Indeed, psychological experiments suggest that we make judgements of each other's social status within the first few seconds of meeting. No wonder first impressions count, and no wonder we feel social evaluation anxieties! 40

1

		10			20	

2

3

4 (4)

   (5)

5

語句 音声は、「英語」→「日本語の意味」の順で読まれます。 CD 2- Tr 27-30

入試基礎レベル

3 **reasonable** [ríːznəbl] ____

10 **immediate** [imíːdiət] ____

11 **tend to** *do* ____

11 **consist of ~** ____

16 **replace** [ripléis] ____

23 **be concerned with ~** ____

24 **boring** [bɔ́ːriŋ]（形） ____

27 **rate** [réit]（動） ____

30 **instead of** *doing* ____

32 **worth** [wə́ːrθ]（名） ____

36 **exact** [igzǽkt]（形） ____

入試標準レベル（共通テスト・私大）

1 **anxiety** [æŋzáiəti] ____

1 **dramatically** [drəmǽtikəli] ____

2 **psychologist** [saikáːlədʒist] ____

3 **threat** [θrét] ____

5 **geographical** [dʒìːəgrǽfikəl] ____

8 **rural** [rúərəl] ____

8 **A and B alike** ____

9 **boundary** [báundəri] ____

12 **now that ...** ____

18 **distinguish between A and B** ____

19 **concept** [kánsèpt]（名） ____

20 **evidence** [évidəns]（名） ____

22 **previous** [príːviəs] ____

24 **ignorant** [ígnərənt] ____

25 **manage** [mǽnidʒ] ____

25 **make an impression** ____

26 **make an evaluation** ____

28 **psychological condition** ____

30 **accepet ... as ~** ____

31 **setting** [sétiŋ] ____

33 **see ... as ~** ____

35 **philosopher** [filásəfər] ____

36 **indication** [ìndikéiʃən] ____

37 **psychological experiment** ____

入試発展レベル（二次・有名私大）

4 **break-up** ____

4 **settled** [sétld]（形） ____

6 **mobility** [moubíləti] ____

13 **superficial** [sùpərfíʃəl] ____

14 **be rooted in ~** ____

16 **mass society** ____

17 **endlessly** [éndləsli] ____

19 **esteem** [istíːm]（名） ____

20 **self-esteem** ____

20 **sensitivity** [sènsətívəti] ____

20 **coupled with ~** ____

22 **self-conscious** ____

23 **overly** [óuvərli] ____

25 **interaction with ~** ____

27 **insecurity** [ìnsikjúərəti] ____

29 **inequality** [ìnikwáləti] ____

29 **heighten** [háitən] ____

36 **immense** [iméns] ____

39 **no wonder ...** …も不思議ではない

39 **count** [káunt] 重要である、肝心である

その他

2 **the last half century** 過去半世紀

3 **evaluative** [ivǽljuətiv] 評価による

14 **non-existent** 存在しない

14 **sense of identity** 一体感

16 **facelessness** [féisləsnis] 匿名性

17 **open to question** 問題である

24 **come across as ~** ～のような印象を与える

24 **unattractive** [ʌnətrǽktiv] 魅力的でない

24 **... or whatever** …とかそういったもの

25 **at the core of ~** ～の中心に

27 **give a good account of** *oneself* よい印象を与える

30 **social status** 社会的地位

31 **equal** [íːkwəl]（名） 同等の人

34 **Ralph Waldo Emerson** ラルフ・ワルド・エマーソン（米国の詩人・哲学者）

段落要旨　各段落のまとめとなるように、空所に適切な語句を入れなさい。（同じ番号には、同じ語句が入ります）

展開	段落	要旨
序論	1	多くの先進国で人々の（①　　　　　）と「社会的（②　　　　　）の脅威」が増大している。その原因の１つに、過去の定住型地域（③　　　　　）が崩壊したことが挙げられる。
本論①	2	昔は互いを知り合う（③　　　　　）で生活していたが、今は近所の人に関してあまり知らない。その結果、私たちは何者なのかということが絶えず問われている。
本論②	3	かつてに比べ、人々は非常に（④　　　　　）が強くなり、他人からどう見られているかに大きな関心を持つようになっている。自分への（②　　　　　）に対する不安感が現代人の精神状態の一部になっているのだ。
本論③	4	人々の間の不平等の拡大が、（⑤　　　　　　　）の重要性を高め、社会的（②　　　　　）への不安を強めている。

百字要約　「段落要旨」を参考にして、本文全体の内容を百字程度の日本語で要約しなさい。

（下書き）　10　20

10　20

本文解説

1　　【省略】

(l.1)　Why have social anxieties increased so dramatically in many developed countries over the last half century, as one American psychologist's studies suggest **they have**?

▶ as one American psychologist's studies suggest (that) they(=social anxieties) have (increased so dramatically in many developed countries over the last half century)「あるアメリカ人心理学者の研究が（多くの先進国において過去半世紀の間にこんなにも劇的に社会不安が増大したと）示唆するように」

2　　【文構造】【分詞の用法】

(l.4)　People used to grow up **knowing**, and **being known** by, many of the same people all their lives.

▶ knowing の目的語は many of the same people である。省略せずに書くと ... grow up knowing many of the same people and being known by many of the same people all their lives となる。

▶ 分詞 knowing, being known はどちらも、かつて人々が成長した様子を説明している。being known は分詞の受動態。grow up knowing, and being known by, ...「…を知りながら、また…に知られながら、成長する」

3　　【have difficulty in ...】【distinguish between A and B】【hold の用法】

(l.18)　The problem is shown even in the **difficulty we have in distinguishing between** the concept of the 'esteem' in which we may or may not be **held** by others, **and** our own self-esteem.

▶ The problem is shown even in ...「問題は…にさえ表れている」

▶ have difficulty in ...「…に困難を感じる、…する際に苦労する」→ the difficulty (that) we have in distinguishing「識別する際に私たちが持つ困難さ」

▶ distinguish between A and B「A と B を識別する、見分ける」。この文では and B に当たる and our own self-esteem が離れているので注意。

▶ we may or may not be held by others の hold は「（考え・感情などを）心に抱く」。
ex. He is held in high esteem.
「彼は高い評価を得ている」

▶ we may or may not be held in 'esteem' by others「私たちは他人から『尊敬』されていることもあるし、されていないこともある」→ the 'esteem' in which we may or may not be held by others「私たちが他人から得ていることもあるし、得ていないこともある『尊敬』」

4　【文構造】【coupled with ...】【come across as ...】

(l.20) (S)The evidence of our sensitivity to 'social evaluative threat', **coupled with** the American psychologist's evidence of long-term rises in anxiety, (V)suggests (O)that we may — by the standards of any previous society — have become highly self-conscious, overly concerned with how we appear to others, worried that we might **come across as** unattractive, boring, ignorant or whatever, and constantly trying to manage the impressions we make.

> ▶ The evidence of ... 'social evaluative threat' が全体の S、suggests が V、that 以下が O である。

> ▶ coupled with ...「…と相まって、…と結びついて」。coupled with the American psychologist's evidence of long-term rises in anxiety「このアメリカ人心理学者が提示する、長期にわたり不安が増大している証拠と相まって」

> ▶ that 節中は、we may have become highly self-conscious「私たちは非常に自意識が強くなっているかもしれない」が基本で、続く concerned with ... , worried that ... , trying to ... はその具体例となる分詞構文の並列で「…に過度に関心を持ち、…だと心配し、…しようとしたりして」の意味。by the standards of any previous society「以前のどの社会の基準から見ても」

> ▶ come across as ...「…に見える、…のような印象を与える(= seem to have particular qualities)」

5　【倒置】【give a good account of *oneself*】

(l.25)　And **at the core of our interactions with strangers is our concern** at the social judgements and evaluations they might make: how do they rate us, did we **give a good account of ourselves**?

> ▶ at the core of our interactions with strangers が文頭に置かれ、S と V が倒置されている。普通の語順は (S)our concern at the social judgements and evaluations they might make (V)is at the core of our interactions with strangers である。

> ▶ :（コロン）以下は、our concern at the social judgements and evaluations they might make「彼らが下すかもしれない社会的判断と評価への私たちの関心」の具体例である。

> ▶ rate「…を評価する」　give a good account of *oneself*「(立派に振る舞って) よい印象を与える」

6　【文構造　他】

(l.30)　Instead of accepting each other as equals on the basis of our common humanity as we might in more equal settings, measuring each other's worth becomes more important as status differences widen.

> ▶ measuring each other's worth「お互いの価値を測ること」が全体の S である。

> ▶ instead of *doing*「…する代わりに、…せずに」　accept ... as ~「…を~として受け入れる」
> equals「(名) 対等な人々」 on the basis of ...「…に基づいて」 as we might (accept each other as equals) in more equal settings「より平等な状況だったら、そうする (=お互いを平等な人々として受け入れる) であろうように」

> ▶ as status differences widen「地位の格差が広がるにつれて」

Newborns swaddled in a blanket are likely to cry when someone opens the blanket ⊛31 to expose them to the cooler temperature of the room. This cry should not be regarded as a sign of fear or anger because it is a biologically prepared reaction to the change in temperature. Moreover, genes whose products influence limbic sites* are not yet active in newborns. Nor should we call a crying six-month-old who dropped her rattle *angry* because this emotion presumes knowledge of the cause of a distressed state. Charles Darwin, who kept a diary on his child, made (1)that mistake when his seven-month-old son screamed after the lemon he was playing with slipped away. The father of evolutionary theory assumed a biological continuity between animals and infants and projected the state he felt when he lost a valuable object on to both animals and his young son. Many contemporary psychologists attribute a state of fear to seven-month-olds who cry at the approach of a stranger and to forty-year-olds who notice a large amount of clotted blood in their saliva. But (2)the states of these two agents cannot be the same because of the profound biological and psychological differences between infants and adults. The infant's distress is an automatic reaction to the inability to relate the unfamiliar features of the stranger to his or her knowledge; the adult's state follows an appraisal of the meaning of the blood for his or her health.

The infant's behavioral reactions to emotional incentives are either biologically ⊛32 prepared responses or acquired habits, and the responses are signs of a change in internal state that is free of appraisal. The structural immaturity of the infant brain means that the emotions that require thought, such as guilt, pride, despair, shame, and empathy, cannot be experienced in the first year because the cognitive abilities necessary for their emergence have not yet developed.

The restriction on possible emotions extends beyond infancy. Children less than a ⊛33 year old cannot experience empathy with another or shame, whereas all three-year-olds are capable of these states because of the emergence of the ability to infer the state of others and to be conscious of one's feelings and intentions. This extremely important developmental change, due to brain maturation, adds a qualitatively new reason for actions, especially the desire to preserve a conception of self as a good person. (3)This motive, which has an emotional component, is a seminal basis for later behaviors that are called altruistic. Furthermore, children less than four years old find it difficult to retrieve the past and relate it to the present and, therefore, cannot experience the emotions of regret or nostalgia. Even preadolescents have some difficulty manipulating several representations simultaneously in working memory because of incomplete maturation of the connectivity of the dorsolateral prefrontal cortex★ to other sites. (4)This fact implies that seven- to ten-year-olds are protected from the emotions that emerge from a thoughtful examination of the logical inconsistency among their personal beliefs. Older adolescents, by contrast, are susceptible to the uncertainty that follows recognition of the inconsistency between their experiences and their childhood premises about sexuality, loyalty, God, or the heroic stature of their parents. The desire to repair the inconsistency requires some alteration in the earlier beliefs and the evocation of emotions denied to younger children. The cognitive immaturity also means that ten-year-olds are protected from arriving at the conclusion that they have explored every possible coping response to a crisis and no adaptive action is possible. As a result they cannot experience the emotion of hopelessness that can provoke a suicide attempt. Hence, we need to invent a vocabulary for the repertoire of states experienced by infants and young children. (5)These terms do not exist.

★ limbic sites「大脳辺縁系（感情・行動を司る場所）」　dorsolateral prefrontal cortex「側背前頭前皮質」

解答欄

1

2

3

4

5

6

語句　音声は、「英語」→「日本語の意味」の順で読まれます。　CD 2- Tr 34-37

入試基礎レベル

16 **relate A to B**

16 **feature** [fíːtʃər] (名)

19 **response** [rispáns]

入試標準レベル（共通テスト・私大）

2 **expose A to B**

3 **biologically** [bàiəlɔ́dʒikəli]

4 **gene** [dʒíːn]

8 **slip away**

9 **assume** [əsúːm]

11 **contemporary** [kəntémpərèri]

14 **profound** [prəfáund]

20 **internal** [intə́rnəl]

20 **structural** [strʌ́ktʃərəl]

21 **guilt** [gílt]

24 **restriction** [ristríkʃən]

26 **be capable of ...**

27 **intention** [inténʃən]

29 **preserve** [prizə́rv]

29 **conception** [kənsépʃən]

30 **motive** [móutiv]

30 **component** [kəmpóunənt]

34 **representation** [rèprizentéiʃən]

37 **emerge** [imə́rdʒ]

38 **by contrast**

39 **recognition** [rèkəgníʃən]

44 **cope** [kóup]

45 **provoke** [prəvóuk]

45 **suicide** [súːəsàid]

入試発展レベル（二次・有名私大）

6 **presume** [prizúm]

6 **distressed** [distrést]

9 **evolutionary theory**

9 **continuity** [kàntənúːəti]

13 **agent** [éidʒənt]

15 **inability** [inəbíləti]

18 **behavioral** [bihéivjərl]

18 **incentive** [inséntiv] (名)

19 **acquired** [əkwáiəd]

21 **despair** [dispéər]

22 **cognitive** [kɔ́gnitiv]

23 **emergence** [imə́rdʒəns]

24 **infancy** [ínfənsi]

26 **infer** [infə́r]

32 **retrieve** [ritrív]

33 **nostalgia** [nɑstǽldʒə]

33 **manipulate** [mənípjəlèit]

34 **simultaneously** [sàiməltéiniəsli]

34 **incomplete** [ìnkəmplíːt]

37 **inconsistency** [ìnkənsístənsi]

38 **adolescent** [ædəlésənt]

38 **uncertainty** [ʌnsə́ːtənti]

39 **premise** [prémis] (名)

40 **sexuality** [sèkʃuǽləti]

40 **loyalty** [lɔ́iəlti]

40 **heroic** [hiróuik]

41 **alteration** [ɔ̀ltəréiʃən]

46 **hence** [héns]

その他

1 **newborn** [njúːbɔ̀ːn] (名)　新生児

1 **swaddle** [swɑ́d]　（赤ん坊を）布で包む

5 **rattle** [rǽtl] (名)　（おもちゃの）ガラガラ

10 **project A on to B**
A を B に投影する、A を B も同様に持っていると考える

13 **clotted** [klɑ́təd] (形)　凝固した

13 **saliva** [səláivə]　唾液、つば

17 **appraisal** [əpréizəl]　評価

20 **immaturity** [ìmətúərəti]　未熟

22 **empathy** [émpəθi]　共感、感情移入

28 **maturation** [mætjuréiʃən]
成熟

28 **qualitatively** [kwɔ́lətèitivli]
質的に

30 **seminal** [séminəl]
影響力の大きい、発展の基礎となる

31 **altruistic** [æltruístik]　利他的な

34 **working memory**　作業記憶

35 **connectivity of A to B**　A の B への接続性

38 **be susceptible to ...**　…の影響を受けやすい

40 **stature** [stǽtʃər]　資質、名声、能力

41 **evocation** [èvəkéiʃən]　喚起

44 **adaptive** [ədǽptiv]　適応できる、順応できる

45 **hopelessness** [hóupləsnəs]
絶望

46 **repertoire** [répərtwàr]　レパートリー

展開	段落	要旨
本論	1	新生児が毛布をはがされて泣くことは、(① 　　　　　)や怒りの表れではなく、(② 　　　　　)の変化に対する(③ 　　　　　)な反応である。それに対して、成人が唾液に血が混ざっていることに気づいたときの心理状態は、血が健康に対して意味することを評価した結果起こるものである。
まとめ	2	感情に訴える刺激に対する乳児の反応は、(③ 　　　　　)反応か習慣のいずれかであり、罪悪感や共感などの(④ 　　　　　)を必要とする感情は、生後(⑤ 　　　　　)間は経験できない。
結論	3	感情の制限は乳児期以降も続く。(⑥ 　　　)歳未満では過去と現在を関連づけることが難しく、後悔の感情を経験することができない。7〜10歳の子どもには複数の感情表現を同時に操ることが難しく、危機への対処を探求するが、その対処法が全くないという結論に達することができないため、彼らは(⑦ 　　　　　)という感情を経験できない。私たちは乳幼児が経験する心理状態の範囲を表す(⑧ 　　　　　)を持っておらず、新たに作る必要がある。

(下書き)

本文解説

■1 【Nor ...】【文構造】

(l.5) **Nor** should (S)we (V)call (O)a crying six-month-old who dropped her rattle (C)*angry* because this emotion presumes knowledge of the cause of a distressed state.

> ▶ nor は先行する否定を受けて「…でもない」。We should not call ... angry, either と同意。nor は否定の意味を持つので、文頭に置いて強調すると、続く語順が〈助動詞（be 動詞）＋主語〉となる。
>
> *ex.* Gandhi did not found a church, nor did he create any specific dogma for his followers.
> 「ガンジーは教会を創立しなかったし、また彼の信奉者のための特定の教義をつくることもしなかった」
>
> ▶ we call a crying ... rattle *angry* は SVOC の文型。a crying ... rattle が O に当たる部分で、「我々はガラガラを落として泣いている 6 か月の赤ん坊を『怒っている』と見なす」。

■2 【attribute A to B】

(l.11) Many contemporary psychologists **attribute** a state of fear **to** seven-month-olds who cry at the approach of a stranger and **to** forty-year-olds who notice a large amount of clotted blood in their saliva.

> ▶ attribute A to B「A（性質など）が B に備わっていると考える」
>
> ▶ この文では to B に当たる部分が to seven-month-olds... と to forty-year-olds who... の 2 つある。

■3 【文構造】

(l.20) (S)The structural immaturity of the infant brain (V)means // (O)that the emotions that require thought, / such as guilt, pride, despair, shame, and empathy, / cannot be experienced in the first year / because the cognitive abilities necessary for their emergence have not yet developed.

> ▶ that 以下最後までが means の目的語節である。
>
> ▶ that 節中の主部は the emotions that require thought, such as ... and empathy で、such as ... に具体例が挙げられている。述部は cannot be experienced。because 以下で「生後 1 年間経験できない」理由を説明している。

4　【文構造】

(l.33)　Even preadolescents have some difficulty manipulating several representations simultaneously in working memory / because of incomplete maturation of the connectivity of the dorsolateral prefrontal cortex to other sites.

- ▶ have difficulty (in) *doing*「〜するのが困難である、困難を感じる」　　because of ...「…の理由で」
- ▶ connectivity は to と呼応して、connectivity of A to B「A の B への接続性」。
  cf. He connected the speakers to the CD player.「彼はスピーカーを CD プレーヤーに接続した」
- ▶ preadolescent「思春期（青年期）直前の子ども」　　manipulate「巧みに扱う」
  representations = expressions of their emotions「様々な感情表現」
  simultaneously「同時に」　　working memory「〔心理学〕作業記憶」
  incomplete「不完全な」⇔ complete　　other sites「（脳の中の）他の場所」

5　【be susceptible to ...】

(l.38)　Older adolescents, by contrast, **are susceptible to** the uncertainty that follows recognition of the inconsistency between their experiences and their childhood premises about sexuality, loyalty, God, or the heroic stature of their parents.

- ▶ be susceptible to ...「…の影響を受けやすい、…に敏感である（= be easily influenced or harmed by ...）」
  ex. The geographic location of the nation makes it susceptible to influences from the cultures of the neighboring countries.
  「その国はその地理的な位置のために隣国の文化の影響を受けやすい」
- ▶ by contrast「それに反して」
- ▶ the uncertainty that follows ...「…の結果起こる不安」
- ▶ the inconsistency between A and B「A と B の間の矛盾」
- ▶ childhood premises「子ども時代の前提」　　heroic stature「英雄的な偉大さ」

6　【文構造】【同格の that】

(l.42)　(S)The cognitive immaturity also (V)means // (O)that ten-year-olds are protected from arriving at the conclusion / **that** they have explored every possible coping response to a crisis / and no adaptive action is possible.

- ▶ The cognitive immaturity が全体の主部、means が述語動詞、that 以下が目的語節。
- ▶ the conclusion に続く that 節は同格節。この that 節は and no adaptive 以下にも続く。「危機に対して考え得るすべての対処反応を探求し、なおかつ適応できる行動がひとつもないという結論」。

73

What is the natural human diet? For centuries, people have been debating the best foods, often making it a question of the morality of eating other animals. (1)The lion has no choice, but we do. A lot of vegetarians say we should not eat meat.

🔊 39

But while humans don't have the sharp teeth to kill and eat other animals, that doesn't mean we aren't "supposed" to eat meat. Our early human ancestors invented weapons and cutting tools to use instead of sharp meat-eating teeth.

🔊 40

And gluten isn't unnatural either. (2)Despite the widespread call to cut carbohydrates★, there's plenty of evidence that cereal grains were basic foods, at least for some, long before they were planted. People in the present-day area of Iraq ate several grains during the peak of the last ice age, more than 10,000 years before these grains were planted. There's nothing new about cereal consumption.

🔊 41

This leads us to the Paleolithic★ diet. As a paleoanthropologist★, I'm often asked for my thoughts about it. I'm not really a fan — I like pizza and French fries and ice cream too much. Nevertheless, (3)diet experts have built a strong case for the differences between what we eat today and what our ancestors evolved to eat. The idea is that our diets have changed too quickly for our genes to keep up; the result is said to be metabolic syndrome, a group of conditions including high blood pressure, high blood-sugar levels, high cholesterol levels, and being overweight.

🔊 42

Paleolithic diets make sense, and it's no surprise that they remain hugely popular. There are many variants on the general theme, but foods rich in protein and fatty acids show up again and again. Meat from grass-fed cows and fish are good, and carbohydrates should come from fresh fruits and vegetables. On the other hand, cereal grains, dairy, potatoes, and highly refined and processed foods are out. The idea is to eat like our Stone Age ancestors.

🔊 43

I am not a food expert, and cannot speak with authority about the nutritional costs and benefits of Paleolithic diets, but I can comment on our evolutionary beginnings. From the standpoint of paleoecology★, the Paleolithic diet is a myth. Food choice is as much about what's available to be eaten as it is about what a species evolved to eat. And just as fruits ripen, leaves change colors, and flowers bloom predictably at different

times of the year, foods available to our ancestors varied over time as the world changed ₃₀
around them from warm and wet to cool and dry and back again. Those changes are
what drove our evolution.

☙44   Many paleoanthropologists today believe that increasingly unstable climates through
the Pleistocene★ helped our ancestors to develop a flexibility toward various diets,
which has become a key characteristic of humanity. The basic idea is that our ₃₅
ever-changing world has eliminated most of the choosey eaters among us. (4)Nature
has made us an adaptable species. Thus, we have been able to change from food
gatherers to farmers, and have really begun to consume our planet.

    ★ carbohydrates「炭水化物」 Paleolithic「旧石器時代の」 paleoanthropologist「古人類学者」 paleoecology「古生態学」
       Pleistocene「更新世」

1
....
....

2
....
....
....

3
....
....
....

4
....
....

5
....
....

6
....

語句 音声は、「英語」→「日本語の意味」の順で読まれます。 CD 2- Tr 45-48

入試基礎レベル		入試発展レベル（二次・有名私大）	
1 diet [dáiət]（名）		*7* unnatural [ʌnnǽtʃərəl]	
1 for centuries		*14* build a case for ...	
2 morality [mərǽləti]			…を支持する主張を展開する
3 choice [tʃɔ́is]		*17* blood pressure	
5 be supposed to *do*		*18* overweight [óuvərwéit]（形）	
5 ancestor [ǽnsestər]		*19* hugely [hjúːdʒli]	
6 instead of ...		*20* protein [próutiːn]	
7 despite ...		*23* refined [rifáind]	
7 cut [kʌ́t]（動）		*23* processed [prásest]	
12 lead A to ...		*23* (be) out	
14 nevertheless [nèvərðəlés]			許されない、受け入れられない、問題外で
14 expert [ékspərt]（名）		*25* authority [əθɔ́ːrəti]	
16 keep up		*25* nutritional [nju(ː)tríʃənəl]	
19 make sense			
20 (be) rich in ...		*26* evolutionary [èvəlúːʃənèri]	
21 show up			
22 on the other hand		*29* ripen [ráipn]	
28 available [əvéiləbl]		*29* bloom [blúːm]（動）	
30 vary [véəri]		*29* predictably [pridíktəbli]	
入試標準レベル（共通テスト・私大）		*33* unstable [ʌnstéibl]	
7 widespread [wáidspréd]		*34* flexibility [flèksəbíləti]	
8 evidence [évidəns]		その他	
9 present-day		*3* vegetarian [vèdʒətéəriən]	
11 consumption [kənsʌ́mpʃən]			菜食主義者、ベジタリアン
		7 gluten [glúːtən]	グルテン、麩質（ふしつ）
15 evolve [ivɑ́lv]		*8* cereal grain	穀物、穀粒
16 gene [dʒíːn]		*10* ice age	氷河期［時代］
20 theme [θíːm]		*16* metabolic syndrome	メタボリック症候群
27 myth [míθ]		*17* blood-sugar level	血糖値
28 species [spíːʃiːz]		*18* cholesterol level	コレステロール値
30 over time		*20* variant [véəriənt]（名）	変形、異なるもの
32 drive [dráiv]（動）		*20* fatty acid	脂肪酸
32 evolution [èvəlúːʃən]		*21* grass-fed（形）	草［粗飼料］で育てられた
33 increasingly [inkríːsiŋli]		*22* dairy [déəri]（名）	乳製品
35 characteristic [kærəktərístik]（名）		*24* Stone Age	石器時代（の）
		25 costs and benefits	費用と便益［利益］
36 eliminate [ilímənèit]		*27* from the standpoint of ...	
37 adaptable [ədǽptəbl]			…の観点から見れば［考えると］
37 thus [ðʌ́s]		*36* ever-changing（形）	常に変化している
38 consume [kənsjúːm]		*36* choosey [tʃúːzi]（形）	えり好みする
		36 eater [íːtər]	食べる人
		37 food gatherer	食料採集者

展開	段落	要旨
主題の提示	1	人間の自然な食事については何世紀も議論され、他の動物を食べることの（①　　　　　）の問題にもされてきた。
主題の展開①	2	人間の祖先は、（②　　　　　）や道具を発明して他の動物の（③　　　　）を食べてきた。
主題の展開②	3	（④　　　　　）も、その栽培が始まるはるか以前から、我々の祖先の基本的な食物だった。
主題の展開③	4	食の専門家は、現代の食べ物は祖先が進化して食べるようになったものとは違っており、我々の（⑤　　　　　）は食生活の変化に追いついていないと主張する。
主題の展開④	5	（⑥　　　　　）の食事は理にかなっており、その時代にならった食事をするという考えが人気なのも無理はない。
主題の展開⑤	6	食物選択においては、どんな食べ物が入手できるかが、（⑦　　　　　）して何を食べるようになったかと同様に重要で、それが我々の（⑦　　　　　）の原動力になった、と古生態学では考えている。
結論	7	古人類学者は、更新世の不安定な（⑧　　　　　）が祖先の食べ物への（⑨　　　　　）を発達させた、と考えている。それゆえ人間は適応可能な種となり、食料採集民から農耕民へと変わり、地球を「消費」し始めたのだ。

（下書き）

10　　　　　　　　　　　20

10　　　　　　　　　　　20

本文解説

1 【分詞構文】【a question of ...】

(l. 1) For centuries, people have been debating the best foods, **often making it a question of the morality of eating other animals**.

- ▶ often making it ... は分詞構文で、ここは and they have often made it a question of ... の意味。it は前半の内容を受けて、「最良の食べ物についての議論」。question は「問題、議題、論点（= a problem, matter, or point which needs to be considered）」の意味で、a question of ... で「…の問題」。全体で、「そして、しばしばその議論を、他の動物を食べることの倫理性の問題にしてきた」。
  - *ex.* It's not a question of whether I should go but when.
    「私が行くべきかどうかではなく、いつ行くべきかが問題なのだ」

2 【build a case for ...】

(l.14) Nevertheless, diet experts **have built a strong case for** the differences between what we eat today and what our ancestors evolved to eat.

- ▶ この case は「（論拠に基づく）主張（= argument）」。build a case for ... で「…を支持する主張を構築する［展開する］」という意味。ここは、「食事の専門家たちは、我々が今日食べているものと我々の祖先が進化して食べるようになったものとの違いを強く主張する議論を展開してきた」ということ。反対する場合は、for の代わりに against を使う。
  - *ex.* He had a good case against her.
    「彼には彼女に反論する立派な言い分があった」

3 【make sense】【it is no surprise (that) 〜】

(l.19) Paleolithic diets **make sense**, and it's **no surprise** that they remain hugely popular.

- ▶ make sense は「理にかなう、納得できる、もっともだ、筋が通っている（= if something makes sense, there seems to be a good reason or explanation for it）」の意味。
  ex. No matter how I look at it, his decision doesn't make sense to me.
    「どう考えたって、彼の決定は私には納得できない」

- ▶ it is no surprise (that) 〜 で「〜は驚くにはあたらない、〜は当然だ」。it は that 以下を指す。it is no wonder (that) 〜, it is not surprising (that) 〜, it comes as no surprise (that) 〜 も同様の意味で使われる。
  ex. He's really smart. It's no surprise he got a perfect score.
    「彼はとても頭がよいので、満点を取ったことは驚くにあたらない」

(l.21) Meat from grass-fed cows and fish are good, and carbohydrates should come from fresh fruits and vegetables. On the other hand, cereal grains, dairy, potatoes, and highly refined and processed foods are **out**.

▶ この out は通例 be out の形で使われて、「(事が) 不可能だ、許されない、(提案・活動などが) 受け入れられない、問題外で (= not possible, unacceptable)」の意味。前文の内容に対し、「穀物、乳製品、ジャガイモ、高度に精製され加工された食物はだめだ」と述べている。

ex. Such a proposal is definitely out.
「そんな提案は全く論外だ」

5 【as 〜 as ...】【about の用法】

(l.27) **Food choice is as much about** what's available to be eaten **as it is about** what a species evolved to eat.

▶ 全体は、同等比較の構文の〈as 〜 as ...〉。Food choice is as much about A as it is about B. は直訳すると、「食べ物の選択は、それが B についてであると同じくらいの程度で、A についてである」。

▶ 〈S is about A〉で、「S の (最も基本的な) 目的は A である」あるいは「S の (最も重要な) 本質は A である」の意味を表すことがある。*ex.* Science is about knowing, not about believing.「科学の目的は知ることであって、信じることではない」

▶ ここも、In food choice, what's available to be eaten is as important as what a species evolved to eat. といった意味になる。【native speaker のパラフレーズ】Food choice depends on what is available to be eaten as much as it depends on what a species evolved to eat. / The reasons that foods are chosen are (1)what is available and (2)what a species evolved to eat, and these are both factors.

▶ what's(= what is) available to be eaten「食べるために何が手に入るか [入手可能なもの]、どんな食物が手に入るか」

▶ what a species evolved to eat の to eat は、to 不定詞の〈結果〉を表す副詞的用法で、「ある種が進化して何を食べるようになったか [食べるようになったもの]」

▶ 2つの節は、いずれも間接疑問、関係代名詞節のどちらにも解釈できる。

6 【文構造】

(l.33) Many paleoanthropologists today believe that increasingly unstable climates through the Pleistocene helped our ancestors to develop a flexibility toward various diets, which has become a key characteristic of humanity.

▶ コンマ (,) の前までの基本構造は、(S)Many paleoanthropologists (V)believe (O)that climates helped our ancestors to develop a flexibility. である。that 節中では、help の基本文型〈help + O + (to) *do*〉「O が〜するのを助ける」が使われている。helped our ancestors to develop ...「我々の祖先が…を発達させるのに役立った」

▶ , which has become a key characteristic of humanity は、非制限用法の関係代名詞節。先行詞は直前の a flexibility toward various diets「さまざまな食事に対する柔軟性」。

One of the best measures for judging the true complexity of a job is how easily it can be replaced by a machine. In the early days of the automation revolution, most people thought that technology would cause jobs to disappear from the bottom up. The factory, it seemed, would be the place this reduction would happen first. (1)Assembly-line workers tightening the same few bolts would be swept away by machines doing the job faster, more efficiently and without complaint. (2)Mid-level supervisors would fare better, since no robot would be able to manage the remaining workforce. Fewer manual laborers, however, would mean the loss of at least some managers. It would only be at (3)the top ranks of the organization that jobs would be safe from machines.

🎧50

To a degree that happened. Robots did replace many bolt-turners, but the losses went only so far. No machine could bring the multiple senses to the job that a human can, feeling the way a car door just doesn't click properly in its frame or noticing a small flaw in a half-finished product. Robots might perform truly automatic, repetitive tasks, but jobs that required complex human skills and the ability to think independently were safe.

🎧51

Meanwhile, one level above the manual workers, the mid-level management jobs started to vanish, as employees required less direct instruction. However, at the top of the ladder, the bosses and executives, whose jobs often called for subtle anticipation of markets and expert reactions to changing demands and trends, did, for the most part, keep their positions.

🎧52

The computer revolution had even greater impact on the workforce by automating the handling of information. This caused the mid-level job loss that started in the factory to [A   ]. While such a development may have caught a lot of hard-working employees by surprise, it was in fact a very predictable result.

🎧53

The vast range of jobs and professions follows a U-shaped complexity curve. At its left peak are the bluest of the blue-collar jobs, the ones often held in the least esteem and usually the most poorly paid. At the right peak are the whitest of the white-collar jobs — very highly regarded and equally highly paid. Most people, however, work in the middle — in the valley of the U — where the jobs are the simplest.

🎧54

Nothing better illustrates how the complexity U-curve works than airline ticketing clerks, low-status workers once thought likely to be replaced by automated kiosks. The next time you're in an airport, you will see just as many clerks as there ever were. While a kiosk might be fine for the individual traveler with a single suitcase, it's no good at all to a disabled passenger who needs help boarding a plane, or to anxious parents trying to arrange care for a young child flying alone. Often, human assistance is the only way 35 to solve a problem, particularly if it requires a little creativity or includes an emotional aspect that calls for a personal touch.

✐55   The jobs at the other end of the U-curve [B   ]. It's here that you find the lawyer reading through documents to construct a legal argument; the biochemist gathering test results and making an intuitive leap that leads to a new cure; the psychologist 40 responding to facial, vocal and physical gestures that reveal more than words can.

✐56   It's only in the lower parts of the complexity U-curve that things are a bit simpler. There, the jobs most often [C   ]. (4)In industrialized parts of the world, the growing ability of computers to do this kind of work has led to a hollowing-out of the workforce, with many office clerks and bookkeepers losing their jobs. 45

解答欄

1 (1)a

(1)b

(2)a

(2)b

(3)a

(3)b

2

3

4 [A]   [B]   [C]

5

語句　音声は、「英語」→「日本語の意味」の順で読まれます。　　CD 2- Tr 57-60

入試基礎レベル

1	**measure** [méʒər]（名）	
3	**cause ... to** *do*	
8	**loss** [lɔs]	
9	**organization** [ɔ̀rgənəzéiʃən]	
17	**employee** [implɔ́ii]	
17	**instruction** [instrʌ́kʃən]	
18	**call for ...**	
19	**expert** [ékspərt]（形）	
19	**reaction to ...**	
34	**board** [bɔ́rd]（動）	
35	**arrange** [əréindʒ]	
36	**emotional** [imóuʃənəl]	
38	**rely on ...**	
40	**lead to ...**	
40	**cure** [kjuréi]（名）	
41	**respond to ...**	
41	**physical** [fízikəl]	

入試標準レベル（共通テスト・私大）

1	**complexity** [kəmpléksəti]	
4	**reduction** [ridʌ́kʃən]	
6	**efficiently** [ifíʃəntli]	
7	**manage** [mǽnidʒ]	
10	**to a degree**	
12	**properly** [prápərli]	
14	**complex** [kɑmpléks]（形）	
16	**meanwhile** [míːnhwàil]	
17	**vanish** [vǽniʃ]	
18	**executive** [igzékjətiv]	
23	**evaluate** [ivǽljuèit]	
25	**profession** [prəféʃən]	
25	**curve** [kə́rv]	
26	**peak** [píːk]	
30	**illustrate** [íləstrèit]	
34	**disabled** [diséibld]	
34	**anxious** [ǽŋkʃəs]	
37	**aspect** [ǽspekt]	
38	**intellectual** [intəléktʃuəl]	
38	**instinctive** [instíŋktiv]	
39	**construct** [kənstrʌ́kt]（動）	
40	**psychologist** [saikálədʒist]	
43	**transmit** [trænsmít]	
43	**industrialized** [indʌ́striəlàizd]	

入試発展レベル（二次・有名私大）

5	**tighten** [táitn]	
5	**sweep away ...**	
11	**multiple** [mʌ́ltəpl]	
18	**subtle** [sʌ́tl]	
18	**anticipation** [æntisəpéiʃən]	
24	**predictable** [pridíktəbl]	
26	**blue-collar**	
26	**hold ... in esteem**	…を尊敬する
27	**white-collar**	
40	**make a leap**	飛躍する、大きく前進する
40	**intuitive** [intúːətiv]	
41	**facial** [féisl]	

その他

2	**automation revolution**	自動化革命
3	**from the bottom up**	下から順に
4	**assembly-line**	組立ライン
6	**supervisor** [súːpərvàizər]	監督者、管理者
6	**fare better**	うまくいく、うまくやっていく
7	**workforce** [wə́ːkfɔ̀ːs]	労働力、労働人口、全従業員
7	**manual laborer**	肉体労働者
10	**bolt-turner**	ボルトを締める人
12	**click in ...**	…にカチッと収まる
13	**flaw** [flɔ]	欠陥、傷
13	**repetitive** [ripétətiv]	反復的な、繰り返しの多い
21	**automate** [ɔ́ːtəmèit]	自動化する
22	**handling** [hǽndliŋ]（名）	処理、対処
23	**loan application**	融資申し込み
23	**catch ... by surprise**	…の不意を突く、…を驚かす
30	**ticketing** [tíkətiŋ]	発券業務
31	**automated kiosk**	自動発券機
33	**(be) no good to ...**	…には役立たない
39	**legal argument**	法律的主張、法的な議論
39	**biochemist** [bàioukémist]	生化学者
41	**vocal** [vóukəl]（形）	口頭の、話された
44	**hollowing-out**	空洞化
45	**bookkeeper** [búkkìːpər]	簿記係

展開	段落	要旨
序論①	1	仕事の複雑さの判断基準の1つは、（①　　　　　　　）による代替の容易さである。自動化革命の初期には、まず工場で仕事は（②　　　　　）から順に消滅していくだろうと考えられた。
序論②	2	実際、組立ライン労働者は（③　　　　　　　）に仕事を奪われたが、それは限定的だった。複雑な（④　　　　　　　）や能力が必要な仕事は奪われなかった。
序論③	3	直接的な指示の必要性が減少し、（⑤　　　　　　）管理職の仕事は消滅し始めたが、熟練した対応力が必要な重役などの大半は、その地位を守った。
本論①	4	コンピュータ革命によって、（⑤　　　　　　）層の雇用喪失は事務の仕事にまで広がった。
本論②	5	仕事の複雑さを示すU字曲線の左端は最も（⑥　　　　　　　）らしい仕事、右端は最も（⑦　　　　　　　）らしい仕事、谷の底辺は最も（⑧　　　　　　　）な仕事である。
本論③	6	航空会社のチケット係はU字曲線の有効性を表している。その業務が自動発券機に奪われなかったのは、障害を持つ乗客などへの人の手による支援が必要な仕事だからだ。
本論④	7	U字曲線の右端の仕事は、知的で直感的な技能が必要な弁護士などである。
本論⑤	8	U字曲線下部の大半は（⑧　　　　　　）な情報収集などの仕事だが、コンピュータの能力が高まり、労働力の空洞化が生じている。

（下書き）

									10										20

									10										20

本文解説

1 【It is ～ that ...（強調構文）】

(l. 8) **It would** only **be** at the top ranks of the organization **that** jobs would be safe from machines.

(l.38) **It's** here **that** you find the lawyer reading through documents to construct a legal argument;

(l.42) **It's** only in the lower parts of the complexity U-curve **that** things are a bit simpler.

> ▶ 〈It is ～ that ...〉の強調構文では、～の部分に強調したい語句を入れる。上の例はそれぞれ、at the top ranks of the organization, here, in the lower parts of the complexity U-curve が強調されている。

2 【動詞の強調】【so far】

(l.10) Robots **did** replace many bolt-turners, but the losses went only **so far**.

> ▶ 強調構文〈It is ～ that ...〉では動詞は強調できない。助動詞 do[does/did] を原形の動詞の直前につけて強調する。過去形では did を使い、Robots replaced ... は Robots did replace ... となる。

> ▶ ここの強調は前段落の Assembly-line workers tightening the same few bolts would be swept away by machines ... という予想を受けて、「ロボットは確かに、多くのボルト締めをしていた人たちに取って代わった」と「予想の実現」を表現している。

> *ex.* We all thought he would win the championship, and he did win.
> 「みんな彼が優勝すると思っていたが、その通り彼は優勝した」

> *cf.* "Why didn't you call me?" "I did call you!"
> 「どうして電話くれなかったの?」「電話したさ!」（「対照の強調」）

> ▶ so far は「そこまで（は）、その程度まで（は）」。go so far「その程度まで（は）進む」(If you say that something only goes so far or can only go so far, you mean that its extent, effect, or influence is limited.) ここの went only so far は「自動化革命による仕事の減少は、ロボットがボルト締めをしていた多くの人たちに取って代わったというところまでで、それ以上の影響はなかった」ということ。

> *ex.* I can trust him only so far.
> 「私は彼のことをそこまでしか信頼できない」

3 【文構造】

(l.17) However, at the top of the ladder, (S)the bosses and executives, whose jobs often called for subtle anticipation of markets and expert reactions to changing demands and trends, (V)did, for the most part, keep (O)their positions.

> ▶ the bosses and executives が主語、did keep が述語動詞、their positions が目的語。

> ▶ at the top of the ladder は文全体を修飾して、「階段の最上部では」。whose jobs ... demands and trends は the bosses and executives を説明する関係詞節で、「彼らの仕事は微妙な市場予想や変動する需要や動向への熟練した対応がしばしば求められた」。for the most part「大部分（は）」

> ▶ did keep（← kept）は動詞の強調の例。ここは「対照の強調」と言える例で、前文の the mid-level management jobs started to vanish「中間管理職の仕事は消滅し始めた」を受けて、「しかし社長や重役たちは大部分が地位を保ったのだった」。

4　【倒置】【hold ... in esteem】

(l.25) **At its left peak are the bluest of the blue-collar jobs**, the ones often **held in the least esteem** and usually the most poorly paid.

> ▶ 副詞句 at its left peak を文頭に出して、主部と述語動詞が倒置されている。普通の語順は The bluest of the blue-collar jobs, the ones often held in the least esteem and usually the most poorly paid, are at its left peak. である。直後の文 At the right peak are the whitest of the white-collar jobs ... も同じ構造である。

> ▶ the ones often held in the least esteem = the jobs that are often held in the least esteem「多くの場合最も重んじられない仕事」　hold ... in esteem「…を尊敬する」　people often hold the jobs in the least esteem → the jobs are often held in the least esteem → the jobs (that are) often held in the least esteem

5　【文構造】

(l.30) (S)Nothing better (V)illustrates (O)how the complexity U-curve works than airline ticketing clerks, low-status workers once thought likely to be replaced by automated kiosks.

> ▶ 基本は Nothing better illustrates ... than 〜「〜ほどうまく…を表しているものはない」。how the complexity U-curve works は illustrates の目的語節で、「この複雑さの U 字曲線がどう当てはまるかということ」。

> ▶ low-status workers 以下は airline ticketing clerks と同格で、この職種の補足説明をしている。low-status workers (who were) once thought (to be) likely to be replaced by automated kiosks「かつては、おそらく自動発券機に取って代わられるだろうと考えられていた地位の低い労働者」

6　【無生物主語】【付帯状況を表す〈with + O + C〉】

(l.43) In industrialized parts of the world, (S)**the growing ability of computers to do this kind of work** (V)has led to a hollowing-out of the workforce, **with many office clerks and bookkeepers losing their jobs**.

> ▶ the growing ability of computers to do this kind of work が主部。lead to ...「…につながる、結果として…を導く」　hollowing-out「空洞化」

> ▶ 無生物を主語にした構文なので、まず直訳してから、次に日本語らしい表現を考えてみよう。「この種の仕事をするコンピュータの能力が高まることが、労働力の空洞化につながった」→「この種の仕事をするコンピュータの能力が高まると、労働力の空洞化が生じた」

> ▶ with 以下は〈with + O + C〉で付帯状況を表し、主節に対して補足説明を付け加えている。ここでは O は many office clerks and bookkeepers、C は losing their jobs で、「多くの事務員や簿記係が職を失った状態で（、労働力の空洞化が生じた）」→「（労働力の空洞化が生じて、）多数の事務員や簿記係が失業することになった」。

The most common conception of deserts and arid lands, as embodied by the 1994 ✎61 UN Convention to Combat Desertification, innumerable national development agencies, and many nongovernmental organizations, is that they are barren, deforested, overgrazed lands — wastelands with little value that need to be repaired and improved. Up to 70%

5 of global arid and semiarid lands are frequently claimed to be suffering from varying degrees of desertification. (1)Yet the word "desertification" has no agreed definition, measures of desertification are not standardized, and it is very difficult to differentiate degradation caused by humans from the effects of drought in the drylands, which makes such estimates of desertification questionable at best. Indeed, academic research

10 has shown for more than 25 years that estimates of desertification have been significantly exaggerated and that most of the world's drylands are not being invaded by spreading deserts caused by deforestation, burning, and overgrazing as claimed since the word was first invented nearly one hundred years ago. This has led a majority of arid lands ecologists to conclude that there is insufficient scientific evidence of large-scale

15 permanent desertification.

Desertification as a concept is extremely important, however, not least because the ✎62 fear it generates drives a multimillion-dollar global anti-desertification campaign that impacts the lives of millions of people. Desertification is also important because it was the first major environmental issue to be recognized as occurring on a global scale.

20 (2)As such, the way that the "crisis of desertification" was conceptualized, framed, and tackled as a policy problem shaped in numerous ways our reactions to subsequent environmental crises such as deforestation, biodiversity loss, and climate change. Global concern about desertification is most commonly dated to the 1970s when a great drought and famine hit the sub-Saharan region with terrible suffering and mortality,

25 and resulted in coordinated global action in the form of the 1977 UN Conference on Desertification. Fear of desertification, though, has driven global dryland policy for much longer, dating to the mid-twentieth century with UNESCO's Arid Zone Program and to various colonial adventures in the world's drylands long before that.

Indeed, before the word "desertification" was invented in the 1920s by a French ✎63

30 colonial forester, western imperial powers had executed many different programs to try to restrain the perceived spread of desert regions and also to try to "restore" the

drylands to productivity according to capitalist goals. Underlying these attempts was a complex, long-standing, and primarily Anglo-European understanding of deserts which equated them with ruined forests much of the time. (3)Examining how these ideas about deserts have changed over the long duration will reveal that many of the worst cases of degradation in the drylands have been the result of policies based on the old ideas that deserts are without value and that desertification is caused primarily by "traditional" uses of the land by local populations. Societies in arid lands have, in fact, lived successfully in these unpredictable environments for thousands of years using ingenious techniques. (4)The assumption that the world's drylands are worthless and deforested landscapes has led, since the colonial period, to programs and policies that have often systematically damaged dryland environments and marginalized large numbers of indigenous peoples, many of whom had been using the land sustainably.

35

40

解答欄

1

2

3

4

語句　音声は、「英語」→「日本語の意味」の順で読まれます。　　CD 2- Tr 64-67

入試基礎レベル		その他	

6	definition [dèfəníʃən]	1	arid [ǽrid]　乾燥した、不毛の
7	measure [méʒər]（名）	1	the UN Convention to Combat Desertification
13	lead O to *do*		国際連合砂漠化対処条約
25	in the form of ...	2	desertification [dizə̀rtəfikéiʃən]
			砂漠化

入試標準レベル（共通テスト・私大）

1	conception [kənsépʃən]	2	innumerable [inúmərəbəl]
			数え切れないほどの、無数の
7	standardize [stǽndərdàiz]	2	development agency　開発機関、開発庁
9	questionable [kwéstʃənəbl]	3	deforested [difɔ́ristid]　森林が切り払われた
10	significantly [signífikəntli]	3	overgrazed [òuvərgréizd]　過放牧された
11	exaggerate [igzǽdʒərèit]	4	wasteland [wéistlænd]　荒地、不毛の地
14	insufficient [ìnsəfíʃənt]	5	semiarid [sèmiǽrid]　（気候が）半乾燥の
15	permanent [pə́rmənənt]	8	degradation [dègrədéiʃən]
17	drive [draiv]（動）		劣化、悪化
20	crisis [kráisis]	8	dryland [dráilænd]　乾燥地
20	frame [freim]（動）	12	deforestation [di:fɔ̀:ristéiʃən]
23	date to ...		森林伐採、森林破壊
24	famine [fǽmin]	16	not least because ~　特に～という理由から
31	restore [ristɔ́r]	17	anti-desertification　砂漠化防止
32	underlie [ʌ̀ndərlái]	20	as such　それゆえに、だから
32	attempt [ətémpt]（名）	22	biodiversity [bàiəudaivə́:siti]
41	landscape [lǽn(d)skèip]		生物多様性
		24	mortality [mɔrtǽləti]　死亡者数、死亡率

入試発展レベル（二次・有名私大）

1	embody [əmbádi]	25	coordinated [kəuɔ́:dineitid]（形）
3	barren [bǽrən]（形）		協調的な、組織的な
6	agreed [əgrí:d]（形）	25	the UN Conference on Desertification
7	differentiate A from B		国連砂漠化防止会議
8	drought [draut]	30	forester [fɔ́ristər]　森林監督官、林務官
9	at best	30	imperial powers　帝国主義列強
14	ecologist [ikálədʒist]	32	capitalist [kǽpitəlist]（形）
20	conceptualize [kənséptʃuəlàiz]		資本主義の、資本主義的な
		40	ingenious [indʒínjəs]　独創的な、巧妙な
21	tackle [tǽkəl]（動）	42	marginalize [márdʒənəlàiz]
21	subsequent [sʌ́bsəkwənt]		周辺に追いやる、軽んじる
28	colonial [kəlóuniəl]	43	indigenous [indídʒənəs]　先住の、土着の
30	execute [éksəkjù:t]	43	sustainably [səstéinəbli]
31	restrain [ristréin]		持続可能なやり方で、持続的に
34	equate A with B		
35	duration [djuréiʃən]		
39	unpredictable [ʌ̀npridíktəbl]		

展開	段落	要旨
主題の提示	1	しばしば、地球上の乾燥地の最大（①　　　）％が（②　　　）の被害を受けていると推定、主張されている。しかし、「（②　　　）」の定義やその測定基準は曖昧であり、学問的研究も、それらの推定は誇張されたものだと証明している。ゆえに、乾燥地の専門家たちは、大規模な恒久的（②　　　）の科学的根拠は十分ではない、と結論づけている。
主題の展開①	2	「（②　　　）」の概念が極めて重要である理由は、（②　　　）への恐怖が世界規模の（③　　　）を推進するからである。また、（②　　　）は地球規模の最初の（④　　　）だったという点でも重要であり、（②　　　）に対する政策や取り組み方がその後の様々な（④　　　）への我々の対応を決定づけた。我々の（②　　　）への懸念は、植民地時代にまで遡る。
主題の展開②	3	「（②　　　）」という言葉が生まれる前から、西洋列強は砂漠地帯に対して様々な計画を実行してきた。彼らは、砂漠は破壊された（⑤　　　）同様に無価値な土地で、その主な原因は先住民族の使い方にあると思い込んでいた。その誤解に基づく計画や政策が、砂漠の環境を破壊し、先住民族を周辺へと追いやった。実際は、先住民族の多くが何千年もの間、巧みな技術を用いて、（⑥　　　）な形で土地利用を行ってきたのである。

（下書き）

						10										20				

						10										20				

本文解説

1 【文構造】【前の節を先行詞とする関係代名詞 which】

(l.6) Yet the word "desertification" has no agreed definition, measures of desertification are not standardized, and it is very difficult to differentiate degradation caused by humans from the effects of drought in the drylands, **which** makes such estimates of desertification questionable at best.

- ▶ 文の構造は、Yet A (the word "desertification" ... definition), B (measures of ... standardized), and C (it is ... drylands), D (which makes ... questionable at best).。

- ▶ D の which は、コンマの前の A、B、C の 3 つの文が表す内容全体を先行詞とする、非制限用法の関係代名詞。which 以下の基本構造は (S)which (V)makes (O)such estimates of desertification (C)questionable である。

- ▶ B：measures of desertification「砂漠化の測定方法［測定基準］」

- ▶ C：differentiate X from Y「X と Y を区別する［見分ける］」。ここでは X が degradation caused by humans、Y が the effects of drought in the drylands。

- ▶ D：such estimates の指す内容は、estimates「見積もり、推定」という語から、数量に言及している箇所を探す。at best「（どんなに好意的に見ても）せいぜい、よくても」。

2 【not least because 〜】

(l.16) Desertification as a concept is extremely important, however, **not least because** the fear it generates drives a multimillion-dollar global anti-desertification campaign that impacts the lives of millions of people.

- ▶ not least は「特に、とりわけ（= especially ; used to emphasize that something is important）」の意味で、not least because 〜 で「特に〜という理由から、とりわけ〜のために」。

  ex. Everyone is affected by the weather, not least the farmers.
  「だれもが天候の影響を受けるが、農業従事者はとりわけ影響を受けやすい」

  cf. not the least 〜は「全く〜でない」。

3 【though】【分詞構文】【date to ...】【long before ...】

(l.26) Fear of desertification, **though**, has driven global dryland policy for much longer, **dating to** the mid-twentieth century with UNESCO's Arid Zone Program and **to** various colonial adventures in the world's drylands **long before that**.

- ▶ though は副詞で「しかし、けれども（= however）」。日本語では「しかし、砂漠化に対する恐怖は…」のように先に訳す。

- ▶ dating to ... は分詞構文。date to ...「（時代が）…に遡る」。and to various ... の to も dating に続く。

- ▶ long before that の long は副詞で、after、before などを伴って「（ある時点より）ずっと（後で、前に）」。that は the mid-twentieth century with UNESCO's Arid Zone Program を指す。

(l.32)　**Underlying these attempts was** a complex, long-standing, and primarily Anglo-European understanding of deserts which **equated** them **with** ruined forests much of the time.

> ▶ A complex, long-standing, ... much of the time was underlying these attempts. の補語の部分が文頭に置かれ、主部と述語動詞が倒置されている。these attempts は直前の文の many different programs を言い換えたもので、直前の情報を先に置き、その詳細な内容が後で述べられている。

> ▶ Anglo- は「英国（民）の、イングランド（人）の」を意味する連結形。

> ▶ equate A with B「A を B と等しいと考える」。equated them の them は deserts を指す。much of the time「たいてい（の時）、多くの場合」は equated を修飾する副詞句。

> *ex.* My uncle was at sea much of the time.
> 　「叔父はほとんど航海に出ていた」

Memo

Memo

Memo

Memo

Cutting Edge Black
Navi Book

カッティングエッジ・ブラック
ナビブック 〔付録〕

検印欄

1	2	3	4	5	6
7	8	9	10	11	12
13	14				

年　　　　組　　　番　氏名